Daddykins

DADDYKINS

Kalpana Mohan

B L O O M S B U R Y
NEW DELHI • LONDON • OXFORD • NEW YORK • SYDNEY

ISBN 978 93 86349 53 8

10 9 8 7 6 5 4 3 2 1

Bloomsbury Publishing India Pvt. Ltd
Second Floor, LSC Building No.4
DDA Complex, Pocket C – 6 & 7, Vasant Kunj
New Delhi 110070
www.bloomsbury.com

Typeset by Manipal Digital Systems
Printed and bound in India by Replika Press

To find out more about our authors and books visit www.bloomsbury.com.
Here you will find extracts, author interviews, details of forthcoming
events and the option to sign up for our newsletters.

So when a great man dies,
For years beyond our ken,
The light he leaves behind him lies
Upon the paths of men.

~ *Henry Wadsworth Longfellow*

Contents

Contents

1

You Were Not Born, Sir

In the morning, Daddykins was buried behind the newspaper, as always, when Vinayagam, Daddykins' chauffeur, observed that the obituary section of The Hindu was growing longer by the day.

'See how there's a lot of money in death these days, Amma,' our driver-philosopher said to me. 'Just one photo and the name of the deceased, and it brings in so much cash for the paper. Naturally, it makes financial sense to devote more space to death.'

I tapped Daddykins on the arm as he sat in his rust-orange sofa. I asked him why he read the obituary section every single morning.

'Just to make sure my name isn't there,' my father said. 'You know, by accident.' Saying that, he laughed until his nose turned red and he came up for air.

~ ~ ~

Daddykins could not eat. On the last day of May, when squirrels gorged on mangoes ripening in trees, doctors drilled a tube into Daddykins' stomach. His tongue had long forgotten taste. He died two weeks later.

Daddykins had always liked to be wished a happy birthday on September 15th, which his parents had told him was his real date of birth. He also wanted us to wish him on October 2nd, the date of Mahatma Gandhi's birth. He believed in his core that he bore a distinct resemblance to Mahatma Gandhi. Those of us in the family failed to recognise it, except perhaps in his inclination towards thrift. In addition, Daddykins hoped to be wished on his 'Tamil birthday', which is the day his birth star, Punarvasu, ascended into the sky, according to Paambu Panchaangam, the onionskin 28-page Indian calendar with a caricature of a three-headed cobra that most devout Hindus still follow.

Daddykins had indeed earned his three birthdays. To hurl his first cry upon a world lit up by kerosene lamps was an achievement in 1923, a year in which over 200,000 lives had been lost to the plague in India. At the turn of the 20th century, child mortality was terrifyingly high and childbirth was a private affair inside one's home in the hands of a midwife. Documents of birth were dispensable pieces of paper against the landscape of poverty and India's uncertainty under British rule. Few people had access to newspapers then. Gossip flitted from household to household in the manner of the rat fleas that transmitted the plague through the shared walls of tightly nested homes. When his family heard about dying rats in the neighbourhood right after Daddykins was born, his mother and his grandparents bundled him up and fled to Sulur, a settlement some twenty miles away from Kinathukadavu, his place of birth. Years later when he enrolled his son at school, Daddykins' father simply concocted a date to suit the school's cut-off for enrollment. A high school certificate with that date of birth carried my father through college and his career in the Indian government.

As a married man in his twenties, when Daddykins went to his native village to obtain his birth certificate, it became clear that the fear of plague may have compromised the paperwork at the time of his birth. The clerk at the municipality office took down details about his parents, pulled out a ledger and thumbed through its pages. He stared at Daddykins, unsure of how to break the news to him.

'I'm sorry to tell you this,' he said, 'But you were not born, sir.'

* * *

In 2012, my father's health began to decline. By June, he had lost fifteen pounds in just three months. He complained of indigestion and unease. A PET-CT scan unearthed a benign pancreatic mass, a serous cyst adenoma in the head of the pancreas, with biliary obstruction. But he refused to go under the knife to have the mass surgically removed. He had lived a good life, he said, and insisted that any treatment, if at all, would have to be non-invasive. In August, doctors placed a stent in his pancreas, through an endoscopic procedure, to allow for the draining of bile and to relieve symptoms of jaundice.

A few weeks after the procedure, Daddykins began to complain of brief bursts of excruciating pain in his innards. Racked by pain one October night, he lost consciousness and became very weak. Vinayagam and my sister, Urmila, rushed him to the hospital. Daddykins entered the intensive care unit following severe bouts of vomiting.

Within ten hours upon receiving the call about my father's fragile condition, I was on a flight to Chennai. My mind reeled from my newly-acquired expertise on the esophagus, the stomach, the pancreas and the bile duct. The long air travel from San Francisco seemed to suspend me in nothingness, offering a bird's eye view of my life on earth, as if I were flying over the square miles, looking down, from six miles away, at the vivid and sketchy parts of my mortal existence.

I was fortunate that my children—then a twenty-two-year-old daughter and an eighteen-year-old son—were old enough to take care of themselves. My husband Mo, a computer scientist in California's Silicon Valley, saw me off at the airport. He had listened keenly as I summarised all his 'to-dos' while I was gone. One of his weekly duties: to water the house-plants while taking care to not overwater them.

In the summer of 2005, I had returned home after my mother's death to discover that Mo had killed a houseplant. He had continued to water it long after it had died. I saw its wilted leaves. I wept for hours afterward. I couldn't explain my grief to my husband or my children. The night before I had flown to be with my mother during her last days, a friend had warned me that time—contrary to the popular claim—never really healed. It only helped blunt the edges of grief. Sorrow and grief are like highway pirates. They lurk in the shadows of our lives, waiting to ambush and choke us just as we think we're on a safe ride to a destination.

I recovered in the year following my mother's death, my sorrow allayed by my father's upbeat self. Daddykins had been widowed at eighty-two, but he led a productive life in Chennai. With the exception of minor health blips that his Man Friday and Urmila nursed him through, he rarely ever gave me cause for concern. In seven years, this hospitalisation raked up my dormant fears over my father's mortality. This felt altogether different.

I was anxious throughout the journey. Would my father be alive when I touched down? Would I ever see him walking again with his friends at Jeeva Park? Would my father, ex-Accounts Officer of the government of India, dictate more ponderous emails to me through his secretary at work—with 'From,' 'To,' 'Subject,' 'Reference,' and 'Yours Affectionately'?

A day later, when I landed in Chennai, I did, however, receive good news. My father was stable. But he would have to remain in intensive care until the infection subsided. After poking around his gullet and intestine with an endoscope, the medical team had concluded that his esophagus and a part of his stomach were corroded. 'Could he have drunk some cleaning fluid, perhaps?' the doctor's office had asked my sister, enraging my fastidious father.

A few hours after I arrived, Vinayagam steered me towards Med-India, the little specialty hospital that poked into the sky right after we crossed the grey stone chariot at Valluvar Kottam. He turned to address me for a second. 'Aren't you happy to be back in Chennai, Amma?' He rarely called the city by its old name of Madras. I had never wholeheartedly accepted its name change to Chennai in 1996. Despite the chaos of this hot, dusty town, the feeling of comfort, whenever I landed at its airport, was instantaneous. I had felt it this time, too, notwithstanding the circumstances of this visit.

'We had a scare but the old man isn't quitting anytime soon, Amma,' Vinayagam said reassuringly as we crawled past another couple of blocks on Nungambakkam High Road. His eyes caught mine in the rear-view mirror. 'But, young ladies, I'm warning you, right now, that Med-India isn't a pretty place. Don't go on, about America-this and America-that. The only reason we chose this hospital is because the big doctor there is an expert in his field.'

Med-India was under renovation. Cables garlanded the building on the outside. Inside, electrical sockets dangled off open wires on walls. The din echoed in the waiting room where the copper ends of wires lashed out like fangs, hanging over the heads of families whose drunken men had succumbed to cirrhosis of the liver. Distinguished men in starched white dhotis and shiny leather sandals waited next to barefoot, inconsequential men in colourful checked lungis, all of them plunked down, waiting, for hours, on yellow plastic chairs right outside the door marked 'Intensive Digestive Care Unit.'

Inside, I found my father fuming. Distressed by the burning sensation and pain in his chest and throat and the intensity of medication, he seemed to have grown barbs. A few hours before my first visit with my father, a woman from the Poison Control Department had stopped by his bed to ask him questions. Foul play could not be ruled out and her job was to understand if there could have been some mishandling in the procedure room before or during the endoscopy.

'These people are accusing me of swigging junk,' he said to me, whining that the doctors were hostile and that no one would hand him his dentures. A four-day stubble made him look crusty. He ranted that the nurses always walked past his bed without even breathing his way. Perhaps other patients were bribing them? 'Just who do they think I am?' he bellowed. 'I begged the staff all night for a cell-phone just to be able to talk to my daughter.'

In a move that took me by surprise, Daddykins then bolted upright in bed. 'Get me out of here right now!' he shouted. 'This place is a prison.' He attempted to slide out of the right side of his thin mattress and growled at Vinayagam when the young man overpowered him within seconds.

Daddykins curled back into a fetal ball on his cloth-covered resin bed and lay there sulking. The inspector couldn't have known that my father was a man with refined sensibilities, one who made and sipped the best South Indian filter coffee percolated from the finest grounds roasted at Amudha Coffee. He went to bed every night in anticipation of the next morning's cup. The inspector had also wondered if Daddykins—who was a fragile 89-year-old man strapped to intravenous medication on one arm and trapped, simultaneously, also by a catheter fastened to his penis—may have slid out of bed and walked into the Endoscopy Room and tampered with the unit. Every inquisition came as a personal affront leveled against him, a Class I officer of the Government of India and a man of status and principle.

A few days later, with the pain quelled by drugs, my father did, in fact, emerge a happier man. Vinayagam gave him a shave. Daddykins impressed all the doctors on duty. He bantered with the nurses. They gave him his dentures and glasses. Daddykins asked for his checkbook and his daily accounts diary to be brought to him. Then he told my sister—his primary caregiver—to bring him his credit card to pay off all hospital expenses.

Eleven years senior to me, Urmila was the chief executive officer of our family. Rotund, with childbearing hips that were wider even than mine, she was the most efficient person I'd ever known, further burnished by three decades in Hong Kong and Singapore. In the time it took the rest of us to merely gauge the situation, she'd already have attended to everyone's needs. She opened, unpacked, packed, dusted, hid, tugged, tore, swept, hissed, mopped, squeezed, soaped, wiped, shredded, compacted, and trashed, without any fuss. It was this quiet execution my father loved the most about his older child, that and her unerring loyalty, even if it sometimes took abrasive forms.

Naturally, that week at Med-India, Urmila knew exactly what my father wanted brought to him from his house. She brought him the cash he had stashed in his almirah in a green unmarked envelope so he could compute his month-end salaries and settle his bills at the hospital. Realising that Diwali festivities were right around the corner, he factored in Diwali bonuses for his household staff. He remembered to deduct the advance he had given to the watchman. He marked down payments for the milkman—720 rupees a month depending on the month of the year, he said, and suggested that we verify the amount against the chart in the kitchen back at home. Then there were the monthly dues for subscriptions to television (380 rupees, he wrote) and those for *The Hindu* and other newspapers, 310 rupees. He paused, between the arithmetic, looked at me with keen eyes and said he must reimburse me, his 'little girl,' for my flight expenses from San Francisco to Chennai, an unseemly amount that he did not want his daughter and son-in-law to bear on his behalf. Then he lay back on his bed before being wheeled away for more tests.

When he returned home from the hospital a week later, Daddykins would seek the routine that had always circumscribed his life. He would crave his filter coffee at 5 AM, go on his walk with friends in Jeeva Park at 6 AM, read *The Hindu*—main, editorial, the obituaries and all supplements, except the classifieds such as matrimonial and cinema—at 7.15 AM, and leave for work at 10.45 AM at the office, a securities company where his boss, Thalaivar, his own son-in-law, had just installed a leather recliner so that Daddykins could catnap, as needed, between work.

Except when he was at work, Daddykins didn't wear his hearing aid, the cost of which Thalaivar never told him because he knew how numbers with many zeroes on their tail heated up Daddykins' accountant brain. Vinayagam became my father's ears as Daddykins began fielding all the wrong questions. At home it was often Vinayagam who answered the telephone, conveying to my father whatever it was that anyone wanted to know in a sharp, slightly impatient tone.

Vinayagam looked nothing like Lord Ganesha, the paunchy, elephant-headed god after whom his parents had named him. He was skinny, like, say, a dark Jesus with short, cropped hair and a mustache. He flew to our home on his Honda motorcycle and rang the doorbell every day at 7.30 AM.

Time and illness had skewed Daddykins' attitude towards him. If Daddykins' household were a car, then his 33-year-old driver was its axle. So everyone knew that if we had any trouble whatsoever, that is, if our Maruti Swift Dzire needed service, or if the car needed filling up and we had to watch the men at the pumps at Friendly Indian Oil station so Daddykins didn't get swindled, or the power went out and the inverter wouldn't turn on, or we couldn't connect to the Internet, or the telephone lines were dead, or the toaster wouldn't pop out the bread slice, or Daddykins' hearing aid beeped in its anemic way, or if the maid called in sick when dishes needed washing, then Vinayagam was the deliverer who always knew what to do.

He arrived daily with a clear bag filled with yellow chrysanthemums and roses and, if they were in season, pink lotuses too, all of which he bought in his suburb of Porur where produce and flowers were fresh and cheap. The roses he arranged on an oval silver plate by a framed picture of my mother. He cleaned the prayer alcove for my father every morning, first removing all the dead flowers from the previous day, dusting off the stenciled, rice-flour *kolam* designs from the prior morning, and lastly taking a string mop to the floor. For years, Vinayagam was not expected to step inside the prayer alcove—or, for that matter, into our kitchen—because he did not belong to the Brahmin caste. But as Urmila said in her glum, wise way—her eyes on a sappy Hindi serial on Daddykins' television, her fingers on Candy Crush on her iPad—those attitudes were practical only for the very affluent or for the very able. 'The rest of us need to weigh our options,' she said, her eyes not wavering from the screen, 'before we brandish our ideologies about caste and creed.'

***

A few days after we brought Daddykins back home from the hospital, in early November, Urmila returned to her home in Singapore. I assumed charge of my father's health and his home.

Chatting after lunch one day, Daddykins, seated on his rust-orange sofa, as usual, reading a letter to the editor in *The Hindu*, with Vinayagam lounging on the floor nearby ready to be of service, we meandered into the topic of his parents and large families of the olden days.

'Given that your father lived miles away from your mother and rail travel was slow,' I said to Daddykins, 'did you ever wonder how they managed to have seven children?'

A bark of laughter erupted from Vinayagam. My father bristled at the unspoken accusation leveled against his mother. 'Are you asking me for details of my parents' sex life?' Daddykins asked, shaking the newspaper vehemently. 'How would I know?' He folded the paper cleanly in the centre. 'I suppose things happened when my father visited during the holidays.'

An exchange with a cousin sprang into my brain from decades past. My cousin believed that the sari—whether it was the traditional nine yards version or a modern six yards edition—was the perfect apparatus for sex. 'The sari is the least cumbersome garment of all,' he had said wryly. 'Remember there were no underpants in those days. Just lift, that's all.'

I had assumed that Vinayagam had only half-processed what Daddykins was telling me in English. But Vinayagam had apparently understood, that too, exceptionally clearly, the words 'sex' and 'life.' And, of course he thought it fit to thrust himself into the conversation at that tenuous moment.

'Listen to me, Amma,' he said, rising from his spot on the marble floor right by the Sony Bravia television that he, like his boss, often watched on mute. He had been laughing at Tom and Jerry's antics. Now he towered next to Daddykins, his right arm raised theatrically in the manner of M. K. Stalin campaigning for Tamil Nadu's DMK party.

'In those days, the husband used to visit his family once or twice a year. First of all, Amma, understand one thing,' he said, 'There were no distractions. No television. No one had money. For entertainment. Or for anything else. They had no work—other than to eat...and...sleep, that is. Life was so simple then, Amma.'

Daddykins leaned back in his sofa listening to Vinayagam's pronouncements. He wore a peeved look on his face because while he held his semi-Gandhian parents in great regard, he and I knew, just as well as his whelp of a driver did, that there was much stronger evidence to their experiments with sex than to their experiments with truth.

2

The Boy Who Lived

One morning the blackboard at the local Jeeva Park offered this advice:

'Listen to your heart because even though it's on your left, it's always right.'

~ ~ ~

By early November, Daddykins was back at Jeeva Park. Every morning, he allocated fifteen minutes to dressing up for his daily walk. He went about it as if he were gearing up to ski the black diamond at Courchevel.

First, he glided into a pair of Gap tennis shorts, hand-me-downs from his grandson in Singapore. Over his shorts he fastened, in slow motion, a hip-belt to prevent a third recurrent hernia. He slipped an ironed Adidas T-shirt over his head. Next, wristwatch pressed in place, he lifted his left arm to his left ear and snapped on the latch, listening as the lock clicked in place. Then, he sat on the low, two-foot shoe cupboard right outside his front door and pulled on dark socks that Urmila brought him from every Business Class trip on Singapore Airlines. He slipped his feet into sneakers that were a size too large for them. On his satiny head—it looked like Ayers Rock except for a stray hair that sprouted because he still showed up for a haircut every four weeks—he pressed a baseball cap from Disneyland. All of December and January, he also wound a red, woollen muffler to ward off the chill around his neck. And always, just before he shut the door, he tapped the right front pocket of his shorts once to ensure he had the brown leather pouch with the house keys. Sometimes, his regimen shifted by a minute or two, due to a coffee-related mishap in the kitchen or a slow inimical bowel. But mostly, this soldier reported for his stroll at the park, even on a rainy day, by 6 AM, and thus, quite naturally, eight days after he returned home from Med-India, he was back at Jeeva Park.

He was barely able to walk one round, a fourth of a kilometer, that first day. As we walked he said that the thrum of life in Jeeva Park rejuvenated him. 'Jeeva' meant 'life' in Sanskrit, he reminded me. He retired to a bench, staying to greet friends and revelling in the cool morning air.

With its central peepal tree and the stone idol of Lord Ganesha beneath, the kapok trees on the outer rim and the tall ashoka trees on the inner rim, Jeeva Park became the constant in the infinite variables of my life as I cared for my father. The park also had its own blackboard for announcements.

November, I noticed, had begun to sparkle with Diwali razzle-dazzle. Walkers talked about where-to-buy-what or how-to-make-what for Diwali. But right in that season of revelry, death made its presence felt, as it always did about once every month and the blackboard reminded us of it. Below a quote by Eleanor Roosevelt—'Anger is only one letter short of Danger'—the blackboard regretted to 'announce the demise of Mrs. Krishnan.'

On the day after a member's demise, the president of Jeeva Park Walkers and Joggers' Association waited by the blackboard. He motioned for walkers to gather. Speakers spoke solemnly about the departed. They bent their heads, praying for the soul before disbanding to walk again. Some walked on, talking about the departed member, about his gifts or her wisdom. One round later, walkers seemed to forget about the departed; banter about the departed's love for tennis unmindfully segued into a countdown of the next day's cricket match. Cricket spilled over into the politics of cricket and then into politics itself. Thoughts of the departed soon departed.

Every morning at 7, the bell tolled in the centre by Lord Ganesha. A *mantra* for peace—for Hindus, Christians, Muslims, Jains, Buddhists, vegetarians, non-vegetarians, non-believers, pretend-believers, the Google T-shirt wearers, and the grumpy ones, who didn't ever let others pass them on the track.

vakra thunda mahakaya surya koti samaprabha
nirvignam kurumedeva sarva kaaryeshu sarvada

O Lord Ganesha, of the curved trunk and massive body,
Whose splendour is equal to a million suns,
Please bless me so that I do not face
Any obstacles in my endeavours.

And thus the day's prayer wound down at the peepal tree.

The daily messages on the park's blackboard as well as the care and concern of his walking friends energised Daddykins as he recouped. He walked another half round every day.

One morning in mid-November, a flash of nocturnal rain exhumed the mosquitoes. They zeroed in on the skin above my ankle-length socks. Daddykins and his two friends trekked a semi-circle and stopped, at 6.50 AM, in direct view of the stone-faced lord some forty feet away. My father prayed, eyes shut, head bent.

'I'm being bitten by mosquitoes,' I hissed against his ear. 'Let's leave.' Daddykins raised his head, opening his eyes. 'A few more minutes,' he said. He liked to watch the ritual bathing of Ganesha. 'Once the *abhishekam* is done.'

'But they're feasting on my ankles,' I said. I looked at his two walking buddies who grinned at my plight.

'That's nature. It's god's plan,' Daddykins intoned. 'We are food for mosquitoes.' He looked sideways at his buddies whose bodies shook in merriment. Then his eyes met mine. 'Just like lions eat deer. Patience, baby.'

I pinched his forearm. 'But I'm about to contract dengue fever,' I said. Unperturbed, Daddykins looked at his friends and then pleaded to the deity, hands clasped in front of his chest: 'I beg you, Lord Ganesha, O Remover of Obstacles, to relieve my daughter who is being eaten alive by mosquitoes.' This was as much sympathy as one could expect complaining about mosquitoes to one born into Daddykins' circumstances. While his childhood seemed inconceivably arduous to me, his eyes would light up whenever we spoke of it.

***

My father told me that the colour green was born in his village in god's own country.

I knew the green: a moss green like the algae splattered on brick walls on a summer day; a putting green like the horizons of paddy flanking a railroad track; a leaf green, like the betel plant madly rising towards the sun; an olive green, like the murky lagoon behind a plantation home; an emerald green dipping between the ridges of a banana leaf; and a sea green of the banks beyond the *puzha* that connected the eighteen villages of Palakkad town.

My father was not expected to live beyond the age of six. One photograph remains from his earliest days to celebrate his triumph. In that earliest picture ever taken of Daddykins in 1934, right about the time portrait photography reached the lower middle-class in India, my father is about eleven.

Known then by the name of 'Rajamani' or 'king's jewel,' Daddykins is sitting tall to the left of his mother while she holds his youngest brother on her lap. To the far right, his brother Anandan stares in the way I remember him even in his twilight years—with a quizzical look in his eyes and a tentative frown, as if he had just observed something odd or funny but dared not talk about it. Below my grandmother, half-lounging on the floor but looking like he's not enjoying it at all, is the third brother, Babu, who, in his later years, would talk and laugh to himself in front of the mirror, lost in the world of his brilliant mind.

My father's first sister Vijaya, eternally concerned about everyone and everything, not unlike my sister Urmila, looks straight into the camera. In later years, Vijaya tortured cashiers at Chennai's G. R. *Thanga Maligai Jewellers* with math formulae that never factored in jewellery labour charges and gold wastage rates. Everyone hesitated before placing a long distance call to Vijaya. She enunciated every consonant and every vowel and every diphthong.

In that old photograph, Daddykins' face had already assumed the gravitas of the eldest child. His shirt looked like one fished out of his father's closet; its sleeves dripped all the way to his elbow, there was no shoulder at all and the shirt collar lay flat against the neck. Not that fashion mattered to this poor family. Krishnamurthy the youngest, probably all of six months old, sat on his mother's lap, beatific and unconcerned and naked below the waist. The studio where my father remembers this as having been shot was a makeshift one in the home of a friend in Tiruppur—a cotton ginning town that has been India's primary supplier of cotton underwear for decades—and in a moment of dramatic irony, my uncle was caught with no cover over his privates.

Family photographs from that era flashed male genitalia because producing a male heir was worthy of an Olympic gold. Families would send each other photographs of their naked newborn males, which would then be put in albums with the boy's name written on the back.

My father's family portrait would thus be the first of a rare few. It celebrated another victorious escape from death. In 1929, small pox almost scorched the life out of Daddykins. He survived, yet carried the scars, which cratered his body and face. Though the

Vaccination Act of 1880 required vaccination within six months of birth, it was not enforced until the middle of the 20th century.

Daddykins spent a nomadic early childhood, often staying in the hamlet of Chennimalai with his maternal grandparents while his father travelled to places up in north India looking for a teaching position. For a time, Daddykins' father had taught science at the Native High School in Palakkad but as expenses mounted, he began to explore opportunities outside the state of Kerala. In 1933, he became a teacher at Dahod in Gujarat, 1200 miles away, three nights away by train. His mother chose to raise the family in Palakkad because her lungs could not tolerate the dry climate in Dahod. For the next three decades of their lives, his father sent money home every month and visited home twice a year—for two months of summer and then for two weeks during Diwali holidays. In his absence, their whole family looked up to Daddykins' father's brother—Periappa—who appointed himself the paterfamilias.

The family settled down in the village of Lakshminarayanapuram, where Hindu Brahmins lived on either side of a broad road called Double Street. The two tiled-roof rows of homes formed a garland around the 300-year-old temple and the village deity, Lord Gopalakrishna, ruled from its centre.

Daddykins' mother grew produce for daily cooking: curry leaves, coconuts, coriander, taro roots, yams, bananas, gooseberries, drumsticks and mangoes. Most of Palakkad was unshorn forest. Reptiles lurked in thickets. Just before harvest season, rice saplings rose over three feet in length. Paddy shoots preened in the breeze on either side of the meandering lane when Daddykins walked to school barefoot, holding a satchel of books and pencils in one hand and a cloth bag with a brass box of curd rice in the other, feeling the mud and gravel under his toes and his heel.

* * *

'How did you not cut your feet?' I asked Daddykins. 'Or get bitten? Your father didn't think you needed chappals?'

'Chappals?' my father said with a laugh. We were seated at the dining table. Vinayagam pottered around the kitchen making our coffee. 'Where was the money for footwear in those days?' I'm sure he was wondering, right then, about how much money I squandered on weekly pedicures at Green Trends Beauty Salon right down the road from us.

'Chappals would have been a luxury item on the meager allowance my father sent us from up north,' he said. 'I went to school barefoot, clad in a pair of blue shorts and a white shirt.'

I asked Daddykins why Ambi Saar School did not mandate a uniform. In the India in which I grew up during the seventies, uniforms were compulsory in both government-run schools and private schools. It was one way to iron out the wrinkles of economic disparity.

No sooner had I uttered the word 'uniform' than a guffaw erupted in the kitchen. Vinayagam appeared in the doorway and giggled all the way to the dining table.

'Aiyo! What are you saying, Amma? Uniform?' he asked, setting a hot stainless steel tumbler of coffee in front of Daddykins. He tapped my father on the shoulder. 'Saar, what is your daughter thinking?'

Both Daddykins and Vinayagam were now laughing at me.

'No uniform in those days, my dear.' Daddykins smiled and set the steel tumbler back in its 'davara' and moved them both away from himself as he always did when he was done eating or drinking something.

'What did you wear inside your clothes?' I asked. I heard Vinayagam cackling yet again inside the kitchen as he got my cup ready. 'A vest? Cotton underwear, maybe?' I liked details. My father needed prodding.

Daddykins shook his head. 'I didn't wear any underwear, if I recall correctly. Why is it important anyway?'

I told him that whether or not he wore underwear in the 1930s gave me a sense of the mores of those times.

Vinayagam set a mug of coffee in front of me. When he made my cup, he always made it extra-hot, rustling up a mountain of foam so it crested up two inches from the rim of the cup and gave me a coffee mustache.

'Trust me, Amma, no one wore underwear,' he said, raising his right arm. He stood in front of the fridge—watching me, I know, for the mustache—a red and white checked kitchen towel still slung over his right shoulder. He stood on his imaginary lofty pedestal, like the statue of the late state minister C. N. Annadurai at the Chennai headquarters of the D. M. K party, where this legendary orator stood carved in stone, an upper dhoti cast over his shoulder, his right arm raised as if he were addressing a gathering of a million people.

'Amma, understand that your father could not afford underwear. Just like me. My parents could not afford it. Do you know how many days I went to school with ragged shorts? And torn shirts? Chappals? *Aiyo!* My parents could not afford chappals.'

'But you didn't get hurt walking barefoot?'

'So?' Vinayagam said. 'In any case, just imagine walking in a village full of potholes through slush and water. Remember, it rained. A lot.'

He tapped my dad again on the shoulder. 'Am I not right, *Saar*?' Daddykins looked up at him and nodded. 'No, no, Amma, chappals would have been a nuisance in that village.'

'I'll tell you when my parents bought me my first chappals,' Daddykins said, talking over Vinayagam, who couldn't object because he always made it a policy to talk over his boss. 'Around 1939. When I'd just started working at the chemistry lab in intermediate class in Victoria College.'

I wanted to know exactly what type of sandals Daddykins wore that very first time. Unfortunately, Vinayagam had to step in with an opinion on that too.

'I know, Amma, I'll tell you,' he said. Then he turned to my dad as he picked up his cup. 'You would have worn the chappals with a white base and blue straps. That was the standard, *Saar*. All of us wore those first. Right?'

Daddykins shook his head. He had no memory, he said, of what his first chappals were. He told Vinayagam that the Hawaii chappal he was alluding to was a much later poor man's fashion statement in India.

Vinayagam often forgot that he was born in 1978 and attended school in the early eighties. Daddykins was in elementary school in the early 1930s. Daddykins had lived through an era that he, Vinayagam, was completely clueless about—a time which saw *Love In Tokyo* hair fasteners, gramophone records, bronze water carriers or koojas, the first Coca Cola bottle, Mahatma Gandhi, giant-sized Marconi radios, rumbling Ambassador cars, black paged photo albums with inserts, Lord Mountbatten, rattan punkahs, the Indo-Pak war, Mrs. Indira Gandhi, bell-bottoms, Pan Am Airways' Jumbo Jet, crimplin pants, the Marina beach stampede, the Land Reform Act of Kerala, Air-India briefcases, terylene pants, nylex saris, sideburns, safari suits, and rubia sari blouses.

In Vinayagam's eyes only one thing united the early years of his own life with those of his boss: their poverty. The rest did not matter. And time mattered the least.

3

Living Small

After Daddykins complained about clocks running anti-clockwise and print sliding off the newspaper, I checked the internet about hallucinations in dotage. I knew it was more likely to have something to do with his medication. Still, I had to check.

One afternoon, I pointed to the big clock on the green wall in his bedroom. 'What's the time now, Daddykins?'

'It's 5 minutes after 3 PM,' he said, from his seated position in the middle of the bed. Seconds later he looked at the clock again.

'Or 6 minutes after 3 PM, depending on any error of parallax,' Daddykins said, quickly correcting himself, 'given the angle of vision from this point on the bed.'

I let the matter rest.

~ ~ ~

I slept by Daddykins' side every night after he returned from hospital. In the first two weeks, he needed help sitting up and walking to the bathroom. In the middle of the night, I'd escort him to the bathroom and wait outside the door. I would help him back to bed, easing him into his pajamas on some nights. Every time, he would thank me, through toothless gums. In the day, however, he was another man altogether.

It began with little things, like the water heater. My father's water heater was a local gadget, as it was in most homes in Chennai, intended for use only in the bathroom. Typically, we turned it on first thing in the morning and left it on for a few hours until the last person in the house had finished using the shower. My father, on the contrary, turned it on just about fifteen minutes before his shower and turned it off the second he stepped out of the bathroom. If guests stayed with us, he watched the switch like a vulture eyeing a deer carcass.

Whenever I called him a miser, Daddykins said he practiced economy because he had grown up during the Swaraj era. He had seen rations on countless things during his early years and World War II. Daddykins still saved all the envelopes he received in the mail and reused them for salary payments to Vinayagam, to the watchman who slept in our apartment building and to Ganga, the sixty-seven-year-old harridan who cleaned our home.

My father's implacable recording of thrift until the finish line of his life baffled me. Head bent over the open page of his 1998 accounts diary, Daddykins often sat on the edge of his bed, writing, in pearly script, any amounts that had been spent in his household on a given day.

One evening, he looked up at me from his perch on the bed when I asked him why he continued to record such infinitesimal expenditures.

'I need to know about what's coming into my hand and what's leaving it,' he replied.

'But it's not even half a dollar,' I said.

'Americans may not need to keep accounts,' Daddykins said, meeting my eyes, sucking in the spittle that had pooled at the edge of his lower lip while he had been looking down at his book. 'But I'm Indian.'

I pointed out—to my own peril—that he could afford more. 'As with the heater,' I said. Daddykins retorted that even though the heater was thermostat-controlled, if it were always on, it would cause the whole thingamajig to explode, causing catastrophic injuries to him or anyone in the bathroom. And then there would be the unnecessary expense of a new heater, he added, as an afterthought.

Daddykins and I had a heated exchange over the matter of the heater on yet another day. That morning, my father had turned the heater off while I was still in the shower. The water had turned cold before I had barely begun to bathe. Livid, I ended my shower quickly and stomped into the living room where Daddykins sat reading the newspaper. I berated him for being a thoughtless Scrooge even with regard to the bare necessities of life. Then I marched into my bedroom and banged the door shut behind me.

I stewed for a time inside the room during which I began to comprehend my own children's gripes whenever they returned home for a vacation. But I also realised how the reasons I'd fought with my parents over the course of my life often seemed puerile, in retrospect. Just as I was about to leave my room to make amends with my father, I heard two gentle knocks on my door.

Daddykins stood outside, a fading silhouette of the grand, invincible man I had grown up admiring. I hugged him for a long time. When I let him go, he chuckled, between sniffles. 'Sorry, baby,' he said, his face contrite. 'Won't you forgive me?'

***

On the day Daddykins was swallowed by the river, he had been a slave to routine, as always. At the back of his ancestral home, the door opened to a cattle-shed reeking of dung and grass. Daddykins and Anandan set out hay for the two cows and drew water from the well for the day's needs for their mother. She was an asthmatic.

Daddykins picked up his clothes from the drying room where they lay soaking up the stench of burning wood from the water boiler by the well.

He bounded down the steps onto Double Street, his Brahmin thread diagonally across his bare chest, his cotton towel and dhoti around his shoulder. Daddykins and his friends from Double Street made for the riverbed, away from the Gopalakrishna temple whose bell sliced the peace of the early morning.

Looking like clones, the boys hurried on, chattering, skipping past homes. Their own sisters bathed at home, rarely coming to the river. For an unmarried girl to not stay home was to stray, especially in the eyes of the widow Thangam, who watched the girls of the village from her *thinnai* on Single Street.

On that fateful day, the boys ignored all warnings about the rheumy river from men returning from the *puzha*. Daddykins' friends stayed back to play on the banks but he proceeded to the water. He floated for a time. The water cradled him. He turned to look at his friends playing *kalli*. Water splashed in his eyes. He lifted his face to the sky. The leaves of the peepal tree stretched and danced in the breeze.

The man on the elephant rock spotted him first. He pointed and shouted, between brushing, his index finger and teeth coated with toothpowder. 'That boy!' he yelled to the men scrubbing themselves, closer to where Daddykins seemed to be swimming. 'Look! He'll die!' Everything happened at once. The swimming. The flailing. The rippling. One man dove in, perhaps not remembering his wife or his parents or his children. He bubbled back up. Daddykins' friends ran to scan the waters. Some bathers propped themselves over rocks. 'Who is it?' A hush. 'They say Rajamani.' A scream. A sigh. A wail. Frantic pleas into the darkening sky.

Later, Daddykins' mother said that their family goddess, Bhagavathi, had watched over her son that morning. Else, how did one explain how her boy slipped from the greedy clutches of Yama, and hovered, for shimmering seconds, in the time warp that sometimes lets a man return from the dead? From the arms of his mother, Daddykins told all the assembled friends and family that he didn't realise the river had swollen so. Or that he'd feel too drained to fight the current anymore.

Daddykins was fortunate that when he was dragged into the *puzha*, its gargantuan mouth spat out two fingers around the bend of the river at the bank of Kumarapuram village. The man who saved him told the people gathered in his *thinnai* that he had glimpsed the lad's fingers for a mere second before his gut told him to just dive in.

* * *

Thalaivar had told his father-in-law to resume work for a few hours a day when he felt fit. Across the country, Diwali marked a beginning and Daddykins decided he should resume work on this special day, at an auspicious hour, when the Mumbai Stock Exchange opened for trading.

Attired in a crisp beige shirt and brown pants, much more frail than the last time he wore his work clothes, Daddykins arrived at the office at Capital Place a little before sunset. Since Thalaivar was spending Diwali with his family in Singapore, Daddykins was expected to sign off on the inaugural Diwali day purchase of a company stock. A box of sweets circulated through the office. I popped one into my mouth. Daddykins eyed the confection rolled with nuts, rose essence and sugar. Then he looked at me through the corner of his eyes. I knew Daddykins longed for something sweet. Halwa. Burfi. Laddoo. Foods of sustenance for my father. For a man who drizzled honey on the sweetest mango, a ban on sweetmeats was worse than the prospect of solitary confinement in a maximum-security prison. I felt heartless as I reminded Daddykins that he could not eat anything rich owing to his condition, that he was on a bland lean diet of mashed vegetables, rice and yoghurt until further notice.

At dusk, all the employees gathered outside to burst a bandolier of firecrackers that Thalaivar had bought for the staff Diwali party. Vinayagam laid out the strip along Chevalier Sivaji Ganesan Road, right outside Capital Place. He lit the wick. Bicyclists stopped to watch. Auto-rickshaws swerved past the splutter of fire. The cigarette ends detonated in rapid staccato fire for several minutes pummeling the air with the acrid odour of sulphur, fire, paper and gunpowder, taking me back to the Diwali of my adolescence when Daddykins set aside a scrimpy budget for fireworks. 'Our father never spent more than fifty rupees in the early sixties,' Urmila reminded me on Diwali morning when I called to say that I was planning to gift our father a bag of fireworks. 'And then it inched towards a hundred, staying there long after I got married.'

When I asked Daddykins whether his poor fiscal allotment was because of philosophical beliefs, he shook his head. Children always wanted to give their parents the benefit of the doubt, especially as they grew older, and so I thought my father had been mindful of the poor children employed at fireworks factories under perilous conditions. Daddykins said that it hadn't crossed his mind at all. 'I just don't like to burn money,' he said, 'because I grew up in poverty.'

I pulled out my present for Daddykins to mark my first Diwali with him in twenty-nine years—a box each of sparklers, pinwheels and flowerpots. Vinayagam placed a glowing sparkler in my father's hand. It crackled into a trail of stars. I caught a million golden showers in Daddykins' glasses and on his face I saw a moment of wonder. It was my last Diwali with Daddykins.

4

Marry Her, Or Else

When my father appeared before his gastroenterologist, the physician wanted to know the names of the medicines that Daddykins ingested daily. 'Shinkora, doctor,' Daddykins said. 'It's for my blood circulation.'

'But why does Vinayagam call it Zinkosar?' I asked my father. He didn't know.

I made Vinayagam show me the strip from the pharmacy. I examined it and checked the internet for clarification.

'Aha! The medicine is, in fact, Gingkocer,' I told Daddykins and Vinayagam. I showed them the information I'd found on it. 'Repeat after me,' I said to them. 'It's Ging-ko-cer. It's an extract from the leaves of the tree called Gingko Biloba.'

'Of course, madam,' Vinayagam said, repeating the name with reverence. 'Gin-ko-sar.'

Daddykins called out to Vinayagam after breakfast the following morning in the same old way, 'Can I have my Shinkora?' Vinayagam placed the peach-coloured pill by Daddykins' teacup just as always, 'Here, Saar, take your Zinkosar.'

~ ~ ~

A few weeks after his treatment at Med-India, Daddykins could not eat his favourite meal of the day. For years, he had relished his breakfast of toast with jam and butter. On dark brown toast he spread salted Amul butter. Over that he smeared Kissan fruit jam, colouring the entire surface of a buttered toast as if it were a wall on which he, the painter, could not afford to miss a spot. He relished each toast to the last crumb. When he was done, a streak of jam hung at the corner of his asymmetrical lips. He dabbed it with a tissue until every sign of his continental breakfast was gone.

When I telephoned my sister about his trouble swallowing solids, she suggested blending toasted bread with milk. Daddykins acquiesced grudgingly to the change in his daily regimen.

One morning, he expressed his longing for another of his favourite foods when Vinayagam placed his breakfast of oats blended with toasted bread, sugar and milk in front of him and went back into the kitchen to make us some ginger chai.

'I want to go to Pizza Hut for dinner one of these days,' Daddykins said to me, taking a sip of his warm breakfast. He cast a swift glance to his left and right. 'I like their paneer tikka pizza,' he whispered. He must have caught the astonishment on my face. 'Yes, I'm having a little trouble swallowing' he said, meeting my eyes briefly before he looked away, 'but I can definitely swallow a slice of pizza.' He was in abject denial.

I recalled how a few days before, he had stared at me as I ate a square piece of Bombay halwa in his presence. My father had always eaten small portions but he craved excellence in every bite. He had raved about cousin Kunju's glistening wheat halwa long after she had died. He heaped encomiums on his sister Saroja's Mysore Pak. On his two-month stay in Paris, he was rapturous over the city's croissants. During his repeated visits to San Jose, he pressed us to take him 'just one more time' for a falafel sandwich at Falafel Drive-in.

I understood his yearning that day. 'Maybe a bit later, when you're better?' I said, patting my father's shiny bald pate. 'Don't forget, pizza is bread.'

Vinayagam was by the dining table within seconds, irritation writ large on his face. Ostensibly, he had heard a taboo word mentioned several times in a minute. I have a pet theory that Vinayagam can hear a green anaconda fart in the Amazon even when he's grinding rice and lentils in my mother's stone grinder in noisy Chennai.

'*Saar*, did you say you wanted to eat pizza?' Our Man Friday now stood ramrod straight by the phone desk on which flashed two cordless phones and two corded phones and an answering machine that my sister had bought for Daddykins, who promptly turned off the answer function on it. Daddykins nodded to his valet.

Vinayagam looked down at my father. 'You cannot even swallow a sliver of watermelon or papaya, *Saar*.' He waved his hands, dismissing my father's request. 'We won't be going to Pizza Hut.' He touched my father's shoulder. 'Not in MY car.'

Stone-faced, he moved next to the spot between Daddykins and me. 'And you, Amma, remember that you are answerable to Urmila Amma in Singapore.' My father's head stayed bent over his breakfast so as to make himself impervious to his manservant's rant.

Vinayagam's insinuation that I was daffy and insensitive with respect to the gravity of my father's condition and that he, Vinayagam, was the only responsible human around the apartment and that Thalaivar and Urmila were equivalent to Lord Shiva and his consort, respectively, further annoyed me.

Later, out of earshot of Daddykins, I told Vinayagam that I was aware that Daddykins would not be able to eat pizza but that, unlike Vinayagam, I didn't want to be blunt when Daddykins craved it so much, and that there was a kinder way to talk to an old man than to tell him that his body could no longer cope with his desires.

* * *

The day they watched T. P. Rajalakshmi on the screen in *Savitri Satyavan*, Daddykins and Periappa's grandson, Mani, first began wondering about love, the sort of love that might make a man come back from the dead. Daddykins found himself more conscious, suddenly, of the bigger boys snooping around for a whiff of girls. Daddykins would not tell Mani that ever since he spotted a girl called Gangu, he had sat at the teak writing desk by the window of his home and written their names down next to each other.

He thought about Gangu every morning before he went to college. He would tell his mother he needed to stop at Periappa's place for this or for that, and his mother would tell him to run back quickly because she'd have his lunch box of rice with curd ready for him. Mani would be waiting for him in the *thinnai*. They waited until a bullock cart crunched towards their *thinnai* ferrying Gangu and her friends to Moyan Girls High School. The boys stood by the pillars until it disappeared from sight.

Daddykins never pitched the idea of Gangu to his parents. His uncle, Periappa, would have given Daddykins no choice in the matter anyway. He was 'Rao Sahib' from the British Raj for his visionary leadership in the world of accounting and the family, including Daddykins' father, obeyed him implicitly.

In November 1943, Periappa found Daddykins an entry-level job as a clerk in the Accountant General's office in Madras. Then, he let Daddykins know, as casually as if he had bought a pumpkin at the local market, that he had also met his future wife on Daddykins' behalf and that from what he could tell, she was a fine girl from a family with considerable standing, vast property and respect among the local gentry. Periappa informed Daddykins that he would be getting betrothed to the girl in May.

Daddykins was shocked by both decisions. He was not pleased about going to Madras, a target in the crossfire of a world war. Japan had just bombed Madras harbour and newspaper reports claimed some people had fled the city in fear. Daddykins trembled with rage as he asked his uncle how he could marry a woman without first casting eyes upon her. 'But Parvati is perfectly decent to look at. With a round face,' Periappa shot back, unused to defiance, not least from his nephew. 'What is your problem? Do you want to marry a movie star? Is that it?'

Daddykins would claim years later that he was never intimidated by Periappa and that he had relented because one's elders were accorded due respect in those days. But his sister Vijaya, who was fourteen at the time, watched Daddykins lash out at his mother the day before the wedding: 'If I like Parvati, I will keep her, else you get to keep her.'

Busloads of family and friends travelled with Daddykins from Palakkad to the hamlet of Parur to attend a grand celebration muted only by the absence of the sound of drums since the state of Travancore was in mourning due to the death of its young prince. On the first morning of his wedding festivities, Daddykins dismounted from the bus to meet Parvati, his fourteen-year-old bride-to-be with a round face. He noticed that his bride did indeed have a face as round and fresh as the roundest gooseberry his mother had ever grown. He saw also her kohl-painted eyes and the painted tails at the end of each eye. The morning he met his bride, Daddykins was, in fact, secretly relieved that the British laws banning child marriage did not affect Parvati who was from Travancore. The prayers and festivities went on for four days.

Every morning and evening, Daddykins and his bride were lifted up by their maternal uncles. They exchanged rose garlands. They held hands. They swung on the *oonjal*, a wooden swing with a rice flour design on it, while their aunts sang songs about gods and goddesses. Women hurled red rice balls in the air to ward off evil, fed the couple mashed banana in sweetened milk and washed their vermilion-adorned feet with scented water.

After lunch, on all four afternoons, the bride and the groom sat on the floor, across from each other, on a woven grass mat, while womenfolk from both families sang. There were endless games symbolising courtship – as if they'd had one. Daddykins pried a coconut from Parvati's hands while relatives cheered for her, begging her to hold on tight and not give in. Then, Parvati smeared sandalwood paste on Daddykins' hands and forearms and feet. He broke a whole lentil papad over her raven black head. He noticed that her hair felt soft and slippery under his fingers and while papad dust settled on her hair, her braid and her neck, their tiny nieces and cousins clapped and shrieked with delight. When the gold chain symbolising their union was placed around the bride's neck and Daddykins and Parvati had smiled at each other, the two parted ways.

* * *

'Like all men, your father always wanted to marry a stunning beauty, you know,' Mani, Daddykins' nephew, said to me when I met him at his house in Chennai. I wondered if he was implying that my mother was not that much of a peach. I suppose he was right. My mother was a good-looking woman with even features but hardly one of those doe-eyed beauties with rosebud lips painted by Raja Ravi Varma.

'Your father had a particular notion of beauty and he thought he had found what he wanted in Gangu, this woman from the neighbouring village. Perfect. Sharp features. Classic lines,' he said.

Mani said he had met Gangu again at a wedding in Chennai a few years before. 'The woman looked ghastly. Haggard. Grey hair. She hadn't aged gracefully at all. In retrospect, I think your dad did very well for himself by implicitly obeying my grandfather and marrying your mother.'

I wanted to tell Mani that my father did well by marrying my mother for reasons that transcended physical appearance. By the time I was born, arranged marriages had evolved. I was thankful that by the 1970s, both the man and the woman had a choice in their partners. A period of courtship following the engagement helped a couple get to know each other so that decisions were not based solely on beauty, education, wealth and other such markers.

When I went back home that afternoon, I asked my father about Gangu. Vinayagam touched his shoulder. 'Was she really, really beautiful, *Saar?*' Daddykins ignored him and glared at me.

'That nephew of mine told you such asinine things? What was the need for Mani to tell you all that from years ago?'

Vinayagam laughed. '*Saar*, you were up to mischief, weren't you, *Saar*?' he said, giggling and massaging my father's shoulders. The young man winked at me and then he began to preach, as usual.

'Truth is, every human being has a soft corner in his place for his first love, Amma,' he said, even as Daddykins got up and stalked off into his bedroom while his leather armchair rocked violently in front of the television in his wake.

5

Madras Central

My father used to frown when my teenage sister vegetated on a rattan chair, her legs on the coffee table. Newspaper splayed over her thighs, she liked to turn the knobs of our old Marconi radio with her toes while listening to Binaca Geetmala. Daddykins often called her a butter-cutter.

~ ~ ~

Through the course of his life, Daddykins managed to brand almost every non-starter a butter-cutter: Urmila, me; Vinayagam; my mother; Gandhi, George W Bush, Federer. On and off, the name was also awarded to his three sisters—called Three Roses by Vinayagam after a brand of tea he bought—Vijaya, who was now in her eighties, Saroja in her seventies, Samyuktha in her sixties, who doted on Daddykins, nevertheless, and called him every other day to check on him.

The Three Roses told me how, in Palakkad, everyone was characterised by a brand: of laziness, of frugality, of shrewdness, of lewdness, of loudness. They mentioned the teacher everyone knew as Mashikupi—'ink-bottle' in Malayalam—who had a short neck over wide shoulders, his torso resembling an ink-bottle of the olden days. A label was a rite of passage for every young man in Palakkad and I suppose it would have been impossible to not have been influenced by a peculiar lot of people. The village assigned Daddykins the prefix of 'dosa' owing to the smallpox scarring on his face.

Names stuck long after people had changed in Palakkad and Daddykins always said that life in the village imbued its people with both a sense of community and a sense of humour. Most of my father's choicest anecdotes traced back to his boyhood. Until my father fell chronically ill, one thing was a daily occurrence in our home. During the telling of a joke, he would clutch his chest in a breathless fit for several long minutes, spluttering into laughter because the joke was always on one of us and funnier still when his victim was not amused.

In the eighties, he pulled off one of his signature pranks on Usha, one of his youngest nieces, a girl born and raised in the state of Orissa, who, Daddykins maintained, was always much too 'gussa,' meaning 'angry,' in Hindi. Like every cousin and grandnephew and grandchild before her, Usha too was ensnared by Daddykins' dhoti.

Whenever he was about to play the dhoti trick, Daddykins waited for cacophony in the house. While the mickle of cousins and aunts and uncles was knotted up in conversation, Daddykins slid out. He walked about the house as if he were engaged in a chore. But all the while he busied himself twisting one end of his fine cotton dhoti such that the thinnest part of cloth stuck out. He went to a faucet to wet the corner of the dhoti. He dragged the edge of his nails over the cotton and sharpened the end of the threads. Daddykins worked the cloth until it was delicate and pointy, like the antenna of a grasshopper. Then he moved about in stealth among the unsuspecting family members, prowling around us as we chatted over coffee and snacks. Suddenly, when everyone was oblivious to him, Daddykins snuck into view, with a soundless shuffle, from behind a pillar or a sofa or a door, teasing the soft, needle end of his dhoti into his victim's ear.

The afternoon Usha's ear was the target, she jumped from her seat, shrieking, covering her ears in fright. And while the rest of us roared with merriment, Usha, laughing and screaming, chased Daddykins all the way into the verandah and down into our courtyard.

Thirty years later, as ill health whittled down my father's muscle mass, he had lost that gift for slapstick and now he resembled a gourd that had dried in its bin too long—no flesh, all ridge.

And yet, so late in his life, I saw my father's caustic wit at work as on the December morning he padded over to the telephone. He eased into the leather chair in front of his phone desk. In slow motion, he turned the pages of his black address book. Notepapers tumbled onto the floor. Vinayagam, always eager to help, wanted to know exactly whom he was calling.

'Ganesan,' Daddykins responded, in a cryptic tone. My father probably felt that access to the information was not necessary for the conduct of Vinayagam's official duties.

'Which Ganesan, *Saar*?' Vinayagam asked, picking up the pieces of paper from the floor. He stared at them for clues. He often told me he never forgot a relative's face, their apartment name and floor number, the design on an apartment door, the direction in which a house was located from the stairwell.

'Which Ganesan, *Saar*?' he demanded again. Vinayagam rarely gave up. Daddykins rarely gave in. 'The Ganesan on Scheme Road?' he asked, again. 'Or the one over on Nachiappan Street?' He paused. 'Or the electrician?'

'Sivaji Ganesan,' Daddykins retorted flatly with a blistering stare at Vinayagam before plunging into a conversation with his nephew on Scheme Road.

The one and only Sivaji Ganesan—South India's Marlon Brando, a schmaltzy actor too famous to have entered Daddykins' address book—had been cremated over a decade ago, in 2001.

***

On a cool morning in November 1943, Daddykins dismounted a tanga outside his cousin's home on Ranga Iyer Street in Madras. He counted out his last few annas to pay the driver. That week my father, then barely twenty years old, would join duty at the local Accountant General's office as an entry-level clerk on a salary of 50 rupees.

Madras Central Station had awed him. He had gaped at its vast interior. Outside, he had marvelled at the building's Gothic towers and Romanesque arches in terracotta and white. From the tanga, he had taken in the sign for 'Murphy Radio,' the clock tower, its flagstaff, and then—as he inhaled the dung-vapour and horsehair of the animal trotting ahead of him—the town's broad roads, its spacious parks, its street lamps and the big shops. And the cars. They sailed like ships. He had counted at least ten cars on the five-mile ride into T. Nagar from the railway station.

'Don't forget to tell my son to drive you to Marina Beach,' Periappa had told him at Olavakkot station the night before, patting him on the back, hurrying him along as the night train rolled to a two-minute stop. Daddykins had waved frantically to his uncle, his mother and Saroja and Anandan.

Now, as he turned to look at his cousin's bungalow, he began to fret. Should he call Periappa's son 'Doctor' now that he was a doctor? Would Kunju, Doctor's wife, be hospitable? He tugged at the latch of the iron gate leading into the garden. He saw the little sign, black on white: 'Doctor is in.' He noted the sweeping verandah, a sit-out for patients with cane chairs and benches. He wondered when he would afford a room of his own.

Kunju made him feel special and welcome in her home. 'My father-in-law asked you to stay here and, here you'll stay as long as it takes you to settle down.' The next morning, he reported to work at the office in Teynampet. Daddykins was shown to his desk in a crowded corner of a bright, noisy room. He could smell the dust trapped between bundles of papers stacked up on tables and shelves.

The monotony of work soon caught up with him. Periappa had thwarted his attempt at working at a small fertilizer factory where he might have used what he had learned in college. As far as Periappa was concerned, accounting was most respectable and his brother and his nephew simply didn't know any better. And so, Daddykins listened and worked hard, often suffering lackadaisical older men who gossiped, chewed betel and bullied their subordinates, and turned unctuous the moment a big boss walked by their desk. Daddykins compared their lack of work ethic to his cousin's sense of propriety.

Doctor was ten years older than him and one of only a handful of physicians practicing in T. Nagar. He was a slight man, not taller than five feet. He lived by the clock. He prayed after he showered in the morning. When Daddykins dined with Doctor and Kunju every night, Daddykins noticed their strict diet: the quantity of rice, the greens, the three-hour break Doctor insisted upon between dinner and bedtime. Years later, Daddykins would tell us that Doctor's military discipline and his philosophy of 'eating to live' kept doctors away from him.

Sometimes, through the swinging half door leading from the patients' sit-out into the consulting room, Daddykins heard how Doctor listened to his patients. Daddykins knew he said very little to his patients and sometimes he sounded brusque, as if he wanted to dismiss the patient quickly. Later in the night, when they talked after dinner, Doctor told Daddykins that the best clinician was one who spoke little, listened the keenest and prescribed minimum medication. Saying that, Doctor would break into his restrained laugh.

Daddykins enjoyed listening to Doctor and Kunju dissect a Carnatic music concert after they attended one with him in tow. On some weekends, Doctor drove Kunju and Daddykins to Marina beach in his Wolseley. They walked on the sand. Daddyins considered that he too could learn, like his cousin and his wife, to be a connoisseur of the good life within prescribed limits.

Doctor had worked very hard, but Periappa had also given him a sprawling bungalow when Doctor was barely nineteen. He had also bought his son a car when he graduated from medical college and built a garage for his car right across the house.

Daddykins' life, on the other hand, was penurious at twenty years of age, until he received, a month after arriving at Doctor's, his first salary. Out of that, he would need to send money home to his mother in Palakkad and also try to carve out some savings.

6

Parvati Makes a Life

Daddykins began subscribing to Ananda Vikatan, a Tamil weekly, so that Parvati would read and learn about the world. He said that even though his wife had not had a formal education, she was a shrewd observer of people and their ways.

In early 1945, Daddykins returned to Palakkad a year after their marriage. Parvati had reached puberty. Now, she would begin conjugal life with her husband while getting to know her new family. A charcoal-burning bus ferried Parvati, her parents and her siblings to the railway station in Alwaye, wheezing across ten rain-sodden miles of a narrow, pockmarked road flanked by pepper vine creepers, jackfruit orchards, coconut groves and banana plantations. The family then chugged through eighty miles of algae green paddy fields at the foothills of the Western Ghat mountains before disembarking at Olavakkot railway station. For the last three miles to her husband's village in Palakkad, the young bride swayed to the ambling bullock cart, riding amid the scent of wet mud, dewy shoots of paddy, hay and dung.

The afternoon Parvati was to arrive, Daddykins waited, light-headed with nerves. He ran to the *thinnai* when the sound of crunching wheels reached his ears but he ran back into the house, seized by an awkwardness he could not explain. He stood wooden-legged by the kitchen, the sound of his heart in his ears. In a few minutes the whole village would throng their *thinnai*.

Saroja ran up to him and tugged at his arm. She ran back to the road to summon the help of her brothers. Then, with Krishnamurthy dragging him by one hand and Saroja hanging onto the other, Daddykins made his way outside, where the beat of a *thavil* drum rattled the pillars. The first strains of *nadaswaram* played the wedding song Kunju had taught him. His mother stood outside, holding a welcome tray of fruit and flowers, smiling and laughing with other ladies of the village. The driver of the bullock cart clicked his tongue and slapped the beast. It stopped moving. He eased down to help unload his colourful cargo.

Daddykins saw his wife's small, henna-tipped foot dangling from the cart, the soft, bare foot he had painted with vermilion less than a year ago. Her silver anklet glinted in the sun. Then, old Gopalu held her hand as she stepped down from the cart. Draped in a red silk sari, she seemed taller and less fragile now.

Someone in the crowd cried out to make way for the child-bride to enter her new home. Then Daddykins' mother and his aunt stood in front of the young couple, holding a plate of water dyed red with vermilion, and moving it in a circular motion as they sang to ward off the evil eye.

Parvati's hand was in his. She was climbing up the steps into his home, right foot first. The couple crossed the threshold decorated just that morning by Vijaya with a white *kolam* outlined in red. Parvati's parents entered the home with trays of sweets fused into conical molds, brass drums of savouries and garlands for the couple. Packed into the front of the bullock cart was a new blue aluminum trunk with Parvati's silk, cotton and *Chinnalampatti* saris. Her father had also loaded produce from his orchard. They were gifts to Daddykins' home: bananas, coconuts, jackfruit, braided jasmine and ripe mangoes. They unloaded other gifts in kind: gold jewellery, a tall silver lamp for special festivals, a brass lamp for daily prayer, an oval silver plate and an ensemble of cooking utensils in bronze, stone, and brass; and finally, they brought in a heaping vessel of puttu—sweet and crumbly jaggery, beaten rice, coconut flakes and cardamom—to celebrate their daughter's coming of age in her new home.

Later that night, for the first time, Daddykins took his wife in his arms but he left her side a few days later to resume his work back in Madras. They began writing to each other on yellow postcards. He wrote that he waited for the day she would make him some rasam. She wrote back that she had just learned how to make rasam with tamarind and tomato. He replied: 'Will you make it for me?' And she scribbled, in thick, blotchy letters, because droplets of water from Babu's hand had made the ink smudge so: 'What will you give me in return?' And to that he said: 'I cannot promise you more than a roof over your head. I've found a temporary place for 18 rupees a month on a ribbon-wide lane called Kasi Viswanathar Street. A cozy 800-square-foot space with a kind landlord.' She wrote asking if the place would be lit up by a bulb hanging from the ceiling. He wrote back in the affirmative.

When Daddykins saw her again some weeks later, he realised Parvati was now just another of his mother's girls. Parvati and Vijaya were constant companions. Every afternoon, the girls, including Saroja, stood under the direct rays of the sun in the *tavaram*. His mother rubbed coconut oil into the girls' scalp, combed their hair with long, heavy strokes and plaited it into a tight raven rope because girls from decent families always braided their hair.

Parvati arrived in Madras in early 1946. Every morning, as Daddykins left for work, she would wave until he turned the corner towards the bus stop. By 5 PM, she would sit at the windowsill. He scanned the open window as he walked down and if he didn't see her there behind the horizontal bars, he'd whistle—two short, shrill bursts, like that of a mynah—and she'd appear above the blue frame of the window, her rice teeth shining in the centre of her moon-shaped, powdered face, dusted and ready to go for a short outing with her husband after she had served him a cup of coffee and tiffin.

Every day after Daddykins left for his work and before she began cooking, she people-watched from her window perch. She told her husband that she loved to hear the bells pealing at the Shiva temple as she looked onto the road. It reminded her of home, of both Parur and Palakkad. It brought her peace. She loved all other sounds too, she told him, especially the bleat of goats and the calls of vendors. She enjoyed looking at bicyclists and the things they ferried and the balancing act it sometimes required. Most of all, she told Daddykins, that she waited morning and evening to catch a glimpse of two college-going women walking down their street because they wore the latest styles in blouses and saris. She would also watch cadaverous priests walking about the neighborhood seeking business at death ceremonies, feeling awful for them. She confessed that sometimes fear gripped her throat about their own lives. Why did those priests look like ghosts? Could this happen to them too? Did poverty really do that to people? Daddykins told her that as long as he could work and Doctor was by their side, they would survive.

Sometimes, in the evenings, Daddykins took Parvati by the city bus to the shops at T. Nagar. At Nalli's Silk House, Parvati would stand outside the glass window, sighing, watching the light bounce off of gold thread on silk. Daddyins would warn her that he could not buy her anything until they came into some money. He would watch as her face fell. He told her they must save to buy more important things, like a radio for the house that would cost about 500 rupees, at least eight times his monthly salary. There was also the rising price of kerosene, the rationing and the inflation, all of which were the fallouts of the world war.

Once a week, he came home early. He told her to dress up. They rode the bus to Marina beach—the sea-breeze does not cost us, he would say—where she would walk with him, past the speakers on lampposts blasting news from All India Radio, all the way to the water's edge. There, she'd wet her feet, lifting her sari almost to her knees. He'd call out to a boy selling lentils flavoured with ginger, green chilly, mango, coconut and lemon. The boy would run down with a paper cone of sundal. Parvati smiled. Daddykins paid him one-and-a-half annas. Then the couple would eat sundal in the salty, balmy air, hearing the waters crash and curl.

When his accounts showed he could spare a few annas, they bought tickets to see a mythological play at Madurai Devi Bala Vinodha Sangita Sabha. There, Daddykins and his woman-child sat enthralled watching song and dance, cooled by the breeze from punkah-pullers travelling with the troupe.

By the end of the month, however, Parvati worried about the state of their pantry. Daddykins obsessed over the price of everything from coffee and grain to kerosene and sugar. As he wrote his accounts diary, she would remind him of an expense he had missed. Whenever Daddykins' cousins showed up to stay with them for a few weeks while they hunted for a job, Daddykins and Parvati remembered how Doctor had helped them. They slept upstairs, snuggling together in the thin strip of landing while their cousins occupied the living quarters below. Late at night, in bed, when the uncertainties of the nation and the civil unrest hovered as shadows on the walls flanking the stairs, Parvati asked Daddykins whether freedom for India would free them from financial worry. He was tentative. But on the night they saw Gandhi, in February 1946 at Hindi Prachar Sabha, he felt reassured. Gandhi spoke of the country's heritage, the need for independence, of the importance of speaking one national language, of renewing faith and confidence in oneself to self-govern. Daddykins saw how Parvati's eyes turned misty after she saw the great man just twenty feet away. As they walked back home, Daddykins told her of the day he had missed classes at Victoria College and joined his college mates to shout anti-British slogans during the Quit India movement. He told her how all the boys at Palakkad's Double Street would fight to read sections of the newspaper to know what Gandhi wanted young people across the country to do. It had all been worth it, this is a great nation forged by great minds, he said, explaining the gist of Gandhi's speech. And then, although the thought had just seized him, he told her of his desire to travel to other parts of the world to see how people lived, to broaden their minds and maybe even to make some money.

Charged after Gandhi's visit, Daddykins, Parvati and their cousins sat huddled around Doctor's radio on August 14, 1947, the eve of India's independence. Eyes shining, they listened to Jawaharlal Nehru's speech: 'At the stroke of the midnight hour, when the world sleeps, India will awake to life and freedom.'

* * *

'Stay in America as long as you can,' Daddykins said while we sat at his dining table one morning. He had issued the same orders on the phone several times over the last three decades. 'At a minimum, your children can gain admission in decent colleges without your having to pay bribes and capitation fees,' he would say. 'Don't return home unless something changes at the centre in India.' Then he lowered his voice dramatically saying that he prayed that no one was wiretapping him, else he'd be counting the bars from the inside of a jail cell.

Like his father before him, my father felt a deep anguish for the country of his birth. Every morning, from behind the centre of the newspaper, he lamented that his nation was being led astray by rogues and bigots. He was angry at India or Pakistan or both, calling the heads of both countries *muttaa pashanga* or *madaiyan*, both of which were verbal daubs that boiled into a concentrate of 100% blackguard, plus 80% schlep, plus 50% jackass.

In Tamil, my father's curses tinkled with life. In English, they turned sterile: blackguard, madman, terminator, woodenhead, lazy fool, imbecile, madwoman. Some couldn't be translated at all.

Some made no sense when translated: in Tamil they meant 'customer of death,' 'pubic hair puller,' and 'midnight umbrella.'

The morning my father told me to remain in the United States, Daddykins had been stewing after reading a news item. It described how some inert politicians had scoffed at the office of the Comptroller and Auditor General, the CAG, the 'supreme audit institution of India' that he had reported to for his entire career.

'How dare these politicians try to rattle an institution like the CAG,' Daddykins cried aloud, dipping his spoon in a bowl of warm oats. 'Shameless fools! No more democracy for this country!'

Vinayagam patted his back, and stroked his neck to steady his nerves. 'Calm down, *Saar*.'

Daddykins waved his pointer finger at me. 'Stay in America. Don't you ever, ever, come back!'

'Don't yell, Saar,' Vinaygam said softly. 'You'll choke, Saar.'

I urged Daddykins to view it from another angle. 'Do you want India to be ruled by a dictator?' I asked. He stared at his bowl for a time before he turned to me. 'Yes!' he cried, stirring his oats, his eyes darting back and forth between his valet and me. 'Remember the Emergency during Mrs. Indira Gandhi's days? For twenty-one months, everyone peed in their pants. That, I believe, is what India needs. Now.' He sat scowling through the rest of his breakfast hour.

7

Death in Kerala

Vinayagam and I were talking about death and condolence and Daddykins' insistence on paying his respects to the dead.

'You know, Amma, in the last many years, I always knew that someone had died when I arrived outside our door in the morning. I would peep through the long window by the door before I walked into the house. The old man would be sitting in his favorite chair, all ready to go somewhere—dressed in a neat white dhoti and a freshly ironed shirt. When he opened the door I would ask Saar who had kicked the bucket. And he would say there was no time to talk and I would argue with him and run to make him some breakfast. Then we would hurry to wherever it was. Your father always said that it would not matter if he did not attend a wedding or a birthday. But one must never ever miss an opportunity to commiserate and condole, he said. That it was one of man's most basic duties for having been born on this earth.'

~ ~ ~

The night before Urmila flew down from Singapore, my father and I talked as we lay on his thin, hard bed. 'I should have followed

Doctor's orders,' he said. In his later years he'd said it to me many times. Perhaps saying it was a sort of atonement.

Seventy years after it happened, Daddykins had never recovered from my eldest sister's death. At almost ninety, with everyone he could blame having been dead for years, my father still believed that he could have snatched Nirmala from the chokehold of smallpox.

In May 1952, when his father-in-law wrote to Daddykins informing him that his child had fallen seriously ill upon arrival at his home in Parur, Daddykins had consulted with Doctor. His cousin had advised him to rush Nirmala to Madras for treatment. Daddykins had dithered and then decided against it.

'I dared not confront my father-in-law to tell him that my child would receive better medical care in Madras,' Daddykins said to me. 'It was just not done in those days.' Daddykins pointed out that there were many superstitions around smallpox. People believed that goddess Mariamman visited in the body of a child to rid the family of evil. No one defied the wrath of the deity. Daddykins said none of the elders in Parur would have acceded to his request to transport a sick child to seek allopathic care. He had also been afraid to challenge the quarantine measures in force in Parur. Daddykins thus left it up to providence.

Now, years later, in the thickness of the night, I heard the remorse in my father's voice for decisions he had made in that calamitous time. As a child, I too had been privy to the stifling traditions in the Parur household where, until the mid-70s, we, the grandchildren, were delivered by midwives in the privacy of the home. Mother and infant were sequestered in a room for over a month—subject to a Spartan diet, ritual ablutions, and rules of hygiene and etiquette. When Nirmala was born, Daddykins was 300 miles away in Madras. He would find out only much later that Nirmala had not been vaccinated.

She was the first grandchild on my paternal side. The first baby and the darling of my parents, my grandparents, aunts and uncles. I found out about her by accident. When I was about four, I had stood next to my father on tiptoe, bursting with curiosity at the magical objects in his almirah. The face of a beautiful baby, composed, yet fragile, had stared back at me from the farthest corner of the wooden cupboard.

In that only portrait taken at G. K. Vale studio, Nirmala was about two. She wore an A-line shift with a rounded neckline; the sleeves puffed out slightly and tightened into a tiny band at the cuff. A frill flared below it. Her face looked clean, without any make-up in the eyes or a bindi on her forehead or a big black spot on the chin drawn of kohl often meant to ward off the evil eye.

'She had soft brown eyes, brown hair and fair skin and was so angelic that it seemed she didn't even belong in our family,' my grandmother had said to me one night when I asked her to tell me all she remembered of my late sister. It was intended as a compliment, for one to be so fair that they looked like a foundling among their family. None of the fifteen grandchildren who followed Nirmala would evoke that sense of wonderment.

When she died, Daddykins insisted that no one mention her name or put her photograph anywhere in the house for the remainder of his life. Growing up I almost never heard Nirmala's name.

That night in bed, it had seemed perfectly natural for Daddykins to begin talking to me about his late daughter, especially preceding Urmila's short visit during Karthikai, a festival to celebrate the daughters of the family. Daddykins told me how in the months following Nirmala's passing, he would often see my mother lost in her own world while Urmila played with her dolls by her side. I told Daddykins how my mother finally spoke to me about Nirmala the year I turned thirty-three.

My infant son had just returned home after surgery to his stomach. I noticed that my mother had been traumatised as doctors struggled to diagnose his condition. She told me then, how, in 1952, she had been terrified to care of her dying child, knowing that no medical help would arrive due to the quarantine. Visitors approaching their infected home had kept away when they spotted the telltale bunch of neem leaves hanging outside the door. While life evaporated from Nirmala, my mother and her elder sister wrapped her in fine muslin and caressed her with a cluster of neem leaves. They tried to keep her cool on the outside. But inside, in her tongue and throat, the virus raged. When the child stopped urinating, her sister told her it would not be long. 'I watched my child die inch by inch,' my mother said that day as I held my son in my arms, her eyes far away in an ill-fated room in the home of her birth. 'I just held her until she let go.'

As Daddykins listened, I told him about the torment on my mother's face on the day that a door long sealed shut had been broken open. 'I often told your mother that if our child was meant to live, she would have lived,' Daddykins said, his voice petering out. In the band of light that streamed in from between the wall-length drapes, his chest rose and fell with the lightness of cotton fluff from the kapok tree.

***

He couldn't believe the power of a tiny ticking heart. The first time she saw Daddykins' butterfly maneuver, the baby bawled in fear. And then every time after that, Nirmala gurgled and laughed, drooling and hiccupping. Seeing that, Parvati told Daddykins to please stop teasing the baby in case she spat up her milk.

Mahatma Gandhi's assassination in January 1948 had sucked the joy out of the first trimester of Parvati's pregnancy and cast a pall over their lives. At that dismal time, Daddykins began believing that Nirmala had brought them good luck.

A year after she was born, Daddykins passed an accounting exam that brought him both a promotion and a salary of 350 rupees. By the time he arrived in Bangalore with Parvati and his two children—Nirmala, born in 1948, and Urmila, born in 1950— he started believing that the bleakest times for both his country and his family were behind him.

As the superintendent of accounts in a different department, he found himself immersed in an adventure—of language, food and culture—while living on Venkatappa Road, a colony of Tamil-speaking Brahmins eking out a modest life. On some evenings, Daddykins took his family to Cubbon Park two kilometres away, walking past Mani Iyer's café where they ate once a month. The four of them sauntered past acres of foliage, past the old red brick façade of Karnataka High Court and beyond the scaffolding that housed the Secretariat, a colonial Indo-Saracenic edifice.

By the time they were ready to trudge home, Nirmala wanted to be carried too, like her sister. For the rest of the walk the parents found themselves breathless. Parvati was irritated about having to walk the entire distance carrying Urmila who crumpled her cotton sari. And Daddykins would not holler for a tanga or a jhatka, which vexed Parvati further. After a bit of an argument, they jumped into a tanga that would cost them a half of an anna. And the horse soothed them all, its clippety-clop putting them in a trance as it trotted through the garden city susurrant with the rustle of bottlebrush, purple jacaranda, and frangipani.

Daddykins didn't know if it were the calm of lawns and sandalwood trees, but in Bangalore, he found himself uncovering new things about himself. He discovered, for instance, that his father's skill came naturally to him. He began to tutor students on accounting principles.

When a minister's son began stopping by for lessons, Daddykins gathered the courage to visit the minister in his home to ask him if he might be able to help his youngest brother enroll at Vishweswarayya Institute of Technology. Daddykins had never before imagined that one day he would be in a position of authority or that he would have a skill to offer in return for approaching someone for a favour. A certain worldliness dawned on Daddykins in Bangalore. It was a long way away from the boy who walked barefoot to school. In 1952, Krishnamurthy landed in Bangalore to live with them and pursue a degree in civil engineering.

That year Daddykins learned his first lesson in impermanence. By the time Parvati and the two children disembarked from the train at Alwaye station one day in early May, Nirmala's body had begun wilting from high fever. The three of them had traveled to attend a wedding in the Parur house.

As the four-day wedding festivities rolled to a close and relatives began taking leave, Nirmala's fever did not break. The first of the pockmarks bubbled into view on her face during the hottest month in monsoon country.

Days later, when Daddykins, unshaven and haggard, arrived at Parur upon receiving a telegram, he discovered his twenty-one-year-old wife in the corner of a dark room, sobbing softly, helpless against the wrath of Goddess Mariamman. Parvati told him that she had given the child coconut water, buttermilk and curd. When Nirmala seemed to recover and when her scabs had fallen off, she had bathed her frail body in water that had been warmed by the morning sun. But the child had suffered a relapse.

Daddykins escorted Parvati and Urmila back to Bangalore that July. In accordance with tradition, no one in the family enquired after the victim of smallpox. No one wrote letters of condolence or solace. Daddykins and Parvati would never heal. They would carry on.

* * *

In early December, we were watching the grand lighting of the holy hill at Tiruvannamalai temple, 120 miles away from Chennai. Shiva's force was believed to manifest every year as a massive column of fire on its peak where, on the evening of Karthikai, a huge lamp was lit. Visible for miles around, the flame burned at the end of a long, heavy wick dipped in a seven-foot crucible of clarified butter.

'The first lighting of lamps began at dawn inside the main altar of the temple,' Vinayagam said as we sat around the television on the evening of Karthikai. 'Watch how the holy hill and everything around it is deep black just before the big wick is lit.'

At 6 PM, just as he said, the peak of the hill came alive with the column of fire. Daddykins turned to Urmila. 'Now you may light the big lamp in our altar.' My sister laid two wicks inside the old brass lamp that my mother had lit every day for fifty years. She held a flame to it.

Urmila and I had heard many tales about the Karthikai tradition in Palakkad from the Three Roses. The women of the village would take a lamp from their home and light it from a wick of the enormous lamp inside the temple of Lord Gopalakrishna. Then they would carry the fire into their homes, lighting the lamp in their prayer room with it, joining each home to the community, drawing from the energy of the temple to power up their homes.

Outside our father's apartment, firecrackers punctured the quiet of dusk. My sister and I lit two lamps at the foot of a bronze elephant lamp, brass lamps with deep, broad crucibles that were gifts that year from our father, one for each of us. We lit two terracotta oil lamps and set them out by our front door, on either edge of a *kolam* outside our front door. In our old bungalow, our mother would line up lamps along the walls and the verandah and the lights outlined our house by night, assuring us of a place where we could be ourselves again, a place that would be a beacon to us no matter how old we were.

While Vinayagam made us pose with our father, shooting a photograph to record the day, the three of us stood together, our watery smiles giving way to the deepest fears about the transience of our lives. I had begun my own life with one truth, as the first hand rocked my cradle, that the life of siblings too was fleeting. And I realised, in that moment, that the day was not far away when Urmila and I would have no one to call our mother or our father and one less of a home to call our own. When that day arrived, we would be lonelier than two green coconuts bobbing in the vast blue of the Indian Ocean.

8

The Things They Carried to Lahore

Vinayagam called my father's night watchman a humourless clod and hissed at him at every opportunity. 'I don't see why we need Watchman, Saar,' he said to Daddykins one morning. 'Just last Monday, when I returned late after dropping off Urmila-Amma at the airport, Watchman was snoring. I jiggled the gate and the padlock and cried out his name. Then I simply climbed over the gate. Watchman lay there like a roll of carpet, Saar. Nothing will wake up Watchman. Not even a bomb from Pakistan, Saar.'

~ ~ ~

On a hot summer afternoon in 1956, when India and Pakistan were still grappling with the catastrophic fallout of partition, Daddykins carted his family and their twenty-two belongings in a taxi from Amritsar to Lahore to take up the position of accountant at the Indian High Commission. The family travelled for three days by train from Madras to Delhi, where they had boarded a train to Amritsar. By the time they reached, the train to Lahore had already departed. Daddykins engaged a taxi.

As they barrelled past flat farms dotted with haystacks, oxen and wooden plows, Daddykins knew his wife was anxious both about the missed train and about the prospect of life in an alien town where she would not understand or be understood. In the train she had accused him of being hasty in accepting the assignment.

Two years after returning to Madras from Bangalore, Daddykins had become restless again and had requested work in a different part of the world. When he received word that he had been assigned to Lahore, of all places, he was apprehensive but also intrigued. He would have to coax and cajole Parvati first about life in what everyone considered enemy territory. The day he showed Parvati the letter that described his posting with the Indian High Commission, Daddykins had tried to convince her by saying that Lahore was once the most cosmopolitan city in the Indian subcontinent. Parvati had shrugged him off. She would not step out of Madras, she said. He told her that Lahore had once been the subcontinent's centre for education. Parvati said she did not wish to hear any more. Daddykins then told her about a certain Punjabi saying—that 'a person who had not seen Lahore had not really lived.' Just imagine, he said. But when at last he told her Lahore was the Paris of the East, her ears had perked up. 'Will I be able to buy those transparent, slippery saris in Lahore?' she had asked, to which he had quipped, 'but of course, fashions have always brewed in Lahore first.'

Now, sitting in the dusty car, he realised he knew less about how fashions percolated through the eastern world than Winston Churchill knew about how to drape a dhoti. The continuing acrimony between India and Pakistan gnawed at him.

The driver prattled on. 'This road—over 2,000 miles,' he told Daddykins in pidgin English, waving his arm through the window. 'From Kabul straight to Chittagong. Built by Sher Shah four hundred years ago. *Aap ko pata hai?*' Soon they began seeing the signs for the Wagah border. The man braked as he saw the line of vehicles slowing down.

Daddykins fretted about what would happen at the border when he presented his passport. What if the border guard asked him something in chaste Hindi? Most of all, he worried about the expensive radio that had been squeezed into the trunk with all their other things.

The Marconi radio wasn't the only precious thing they carried. They had the Rukmini cooker Parvati couldn't do without. They carried a hold-all that bundled up all the bedding they would ever need and two small cloth bags, one each of rice and tuar daal. They carried their only clothes inside two metal trunks, lockable in front: Parvati's seven saris, her four petticoats, her blouses in cotton in ten different colours, Urmila's five cotton frocks, her favourite coloured ribbons, her school satchel, Daddykins' six white work shirts, four dark pants, a formal business suit in grey and a Nehru jacket in black. They carried their toiletries besides a brass holder of homemade kajal, a silver container of sindoor for Parvati's forehead, for who knew what they would get in a Muslim nation? They carried their doubts about personal safety. They carried their biases. They carried their sorrow and their hope of finding solace.

Daddykins snapped at the customs officials when they refused to allow his radio into the country. They would not release it, they said, without a permit from the Indian High Commission. Leaving the radio at customs, the family trundled back into the taxi. Parvati, her face taut, sat in the back. Urmila lay pressed against her mother. A metal trunk and several bags were piled up high on the seat to Parvati's left. Daddykins sat immobile in front. The driver clammed up. Neither the driver nor passengers reacted to the sights that accosted them on all sides on Mall Road en route to their quarters at Anand Road.

That night, as they lay down on their charpoy outside the house to stave off the heat of the Lahore summer, Parvati told Daddykins that she didn't get a good feeling about their assignment. Daddykins told her to be patient. 'Don't judge Lahore in a day,' he said and asked her to look up at the stars above. 'They're the same ones we saw over Madras,' he said. 'Aren't they beautiful?' The following day, Daddykins took a bus and procured the radio after he produced a permit from the High Commission.

They would encounter other obstacles. When Daddykins began seeking the friendship of those who were different from them, who spoke a different language and, in some cases, embraced another religion, Parvati told him she was uncomfortable around people whose language she couldn't speak. He told her she must change, that there were other ways to communicate—with one's eyes, with one's hands, with a smile. But when Parvati refused to join him and Urmila on picnics with colleagues, Daddykins let her be. She was happiest inside the house.

There were many other things Daddykins could do nothing about. Every Indian working in Pakistan was considered a spy. One morning when they jumped into a tanga to visit Badshahi mosque, a man remained in the shadows watching them while they got off the tanga and slipped inside the mosque; on their return, he was still outside on his motorcycle, waiting. Soon they noticed they were being followed everywhere.

Then there was the problem with letters. Every letter they received had already been opened. Parvati told Daddykins that sometimes it was impossible for her to appreciate the beauty of Shalimar gardens or the Lahore Museum when they were like prisoners in a glass cage. On some evenings, he too felt low, like Parvati, when thoughts of Nirmala seeped in and leached all joy out of their day. On other evenings, his work weighed him down, especially when he had just spent a day with the families at the rehabilitation centers of Hindu refugees to be transported to India. He told Parvati the stories he heard from people—of massacre and loss, of men and women trying to locate relatives after they had lost them during the migration following partition.

On some nights, as they lay looking up at the stars with Urmila curled up by their side, he told her of infants left to die on the road to freedom, of the rape of women in villages, of Sikh fathers slaying their daughters to save them from the dishonor of rape.

But the novelty of the town soon drew in Parvati, too. Daddykins discovered that she was enchanted by the hullabaloo of the two-hundred-year-old Anarkali Bazaar where she loved to haggle. Inside the souk, Urmila begged Daddykins to tell her, just one more time, the story of the slave girl named Anarkali, who was buried alive three centuries before by order of the Mughal emperor Akbar for her love affair with the Emperor's son, Salim.

Political tensions spilled into their homes, too, on occasion. At the Indian High Commission one evening, while the crowds shouted slogans over their frustrations about the détente over Kashmir, Daddykins and all the Indians in their quarters sat inside locked homes fearing an escalating situation.

When their assignment came to an end at the end of two years, ironically enough, Parvati didn't want to leave Lahore. Isn't it strange, she said to Daddykins one night, that even though she had never ever wanted to venture out of south India, she would so miss their visits to the Golden Temple in Amritsar, the food at the gurdwara, the parks in Lahore, the beauty of the winter season up in the north and the taste of dried fruits and, oh, the sweetest grapes, apples, oranges, plums and apricots. The quality of fresh produce up in the north, especially in winter, had elevated her cooking to new heights, Parvati said. Then she told him how fluent their child was in both Hindi and Punjabi, arguing like a local with Soshi and Ganju and her other friends. They couldn't let her forsake all that, could they? And where else but in Lahore would one see such exquisite phulkari and chikan and resham work on fabric? Why go back at all, Parvati asked Daddykins. Most of all, she said, with a smile meant to entice, she would forever miss sleeping on a charpoy in the silence of a moonless summer night.

* * *

Vinayagam complained about every one of my father's retinue of household help. The cook was always under surveillance. He snooped on Ganga like a hawk although she snipped his tail when she got the chance. Another young man known to our family, Saravanan, cared for my father at night just so Daddykins didn't fall and hurt himself. Vinayagam supervised him too.

Vinayagam was just always on high military alert. Now, his eternal vigilant state was impinging upon my father's need for privacy. Following Daddykins' return from the hospital, Vinayagam expected to be informed about every minutia of my father's alimentary health because he varied the old man's diet depending on how his stomach was doing on a given day. Vinayagam was trying to help but Daddykins lamented that he had become a prisoner in his own home. I sensed his vexation. He was being stripped of his dignity by the people closest to him just because he wasn't as physically agile as he used to be. Aging and ill-health had made public the most private of his bodily functions.

I remember the morning Vinayagam followed him to the bathroom door asking him what he was going to do inside.

'I will not know,' Daddykins shot back, 'until I see what exactly I go.' He banged the door shut behind him and fired verbal artillery from inside. 'I don't have the freedom to go to the bathroom in my own damned house?'

Vinayagam parked himself right outside the bathroom door. 'What are you doing, *Saar*?' he asked once again.

He asked Daddykins whether his boss had done 'the small job,' 1, or 'the big job,' 2. When at last Daddykins came out of the bathroom and his Man Friday accosted him yet again, my father poised himself, for a few seconds, on the bathroom mat. 'One-and-a-half,' Daddykins shot back, as he pulled the bathroom door shut and marched through the bedroom door to his rust-orange sofa in the living room.

9

Bungalow in Chennai

It could be hard to tell the rare manoranjitham blossom from the leaves of the creeper by sight. It was the scent —a sickly sweet rush, like the first stab of love—that cast its spell on everyone who passed by the tree. One morning when street urchins, rod in hand, lusted after a manoranjitham flower, my father crept up from inside our courtyard. He pulled the other end of the rod, not letting go until they gave in and fled.

~ ~ ~

On every visit to Chennai, Vinayagam would drive me down to where my father built our first house in 1961. In T. Nagar, where Daddykins had always lived, were world famous jewellery houses and silk sari institutions, kitchen stores, flour-mills, roadside jasmine vendors, one-stop grocery kiosks peddling sundries and people. And people. People crossing right where they might flatten, like papad. People chasing buses on which humans hung, like leeches to skin.

To arrive at the bungalow, we cruised away from Jeeva Park and turned left at the TASMAC wine shop outside which young men peed into the early hours. Our Maruti Swift hurtled down

Habibullah Road, once a broad, shady road with vast homes set behind wide porticos. We made a right turn down North Usman Road, passing Shine Drug House whose manager, Balakrishnan, had prescribed antibiotics over the counter for my father and our neighbours until he sold the pharmacy a few years ago.

To locate our first home, we veered left into the lane called Parthasarathypuram Road abutting Uthra Photo Studio, which hadn't pulled down its shutters even though the business must have dipped into the negative after the invasion of digital technology. I held my breath as our car propelled another fifty feet, approaching the six-storey high-rise, slathered in pastel pink and secured by a tall black iron gate, its rails tipped in gold, as if it were guarding the inmates of Buckingham Palace. It was once where my father's humble one-storey bungalow grew.

* * *

In August 1958, in the month actress Nargis Dutt graced the centerfold of *Filmfare* upon winning the best actress title for *Mother India*, Daddykins returned to Chennai from Lahore, a man on a mission. He was suddenly seized by the desire to own a home.

He purchased a 4,400 square-foot tract of land in T. Nagar for 3,200 rupees from a coconut orchard owner. A mile due north of Panagal Park, the property was not more than a fifteen-minute walk to Doctor's home en route to which they often stopped at Panagal Park. There, Daddykins bought Urmila hot, roasted peanuts in a paper cone, a treat without which she never left the park.

With a cash gift from his father-in-law and a housing loan adding up to 25,000 rupees—when he had never spent a paisa more than he could afford—Daddykins began building their dream home in 1960. A truck arrived, carrying teak and kino wood from Palakkad, a father's gift to his firstborn from his lands by the river.

Daddykins began noticing that everything in life cost exponentially more than what was originally assumed. Moreover, his wife, who never compromised on quality, wanted something done a certain way and that precise way was much dearer for him.

She craved a long window at the landing that would let the sun in. She needed shelves under the stairs for shoes and sandals. Soon enough it began to sound very good to him too, Parvati's dream of an expansive attic over the kitchen, measuring four feet by ten feet by eight feet, a vast one where she would house old trunks, fans, bedding, brass lamps, all her Navarathri dolls, bronze vessels and gigantic copper urns.

While my mother would not renege on her principle that if she had to do something at all, she had to do it well, Daddykins made it clear that he could not stretch himself with a second loan. While they were caught in that tug of war between the sweetness of a dream and the soreness of reality, Daddykins began to feel the pull of the material. He too wanted something for himself, especially after a childhood of nothing.

Daddykins wanted a sit-out in the verandah where he would read *The Hindu*. He imagined a mosaic slab-bench—about eight feet long, two feet wide and four inches thick—for which Parvati had chosen, in her mind, a reddish pink colour with white chips. Daddykins had just bought a scooter, a Lambretta, that he wished to park under a cantilevered shade and so, he designed the shade on paper and had it built with help from a cousin. But in the end, he was most vain about the conversation piece in his verandah—a massive concrete pillar painted in red oxide implemented by a creative engineer. For the next thirty-three years, the red pillar buttressing the slab-bench distinguished Daddykins' home from the others on the road.

When the house had swollen from imagination to soil, he and his wife, now expecting another child, climbed up to their terrace and breathed in the salt air and the tanginess of lime and mango swaying far into the horizon. They saw their own ripened garden shooting into the sky, flushed with Banganappalli mangoes and coconuts. They heard the train rumble into Kodambakkam station a quarter mile away. Here and there, among paddy fields and coconut groves, a bungalow with a verandah and a courtyard blotted the green vistas all the way from Panagal Park to Parthasarathypuram Road. They saw how, soon after the blazing summer days of April but just before the southwest monsoons broke in June, cotton pods exploded at the seam, dotting kapok trees in white fluff. Sticky white fuzz floated down, lining roads, windows and leaves.

Daddykins would always talk about the inscrutability of the year 1961. Unexpectedly, he had been promoted to the post of an assistant accounts officer at a salary of 600 rupees. Parvati gave birth to a baby girl—me—in Parur in October. He wondered, sometimes, if Nirmala had been reborn in my form. Fate is strange. In that lucky year, my father's face was also marred for life.

One morning, while Daddykins was riding his bicycle to work, a bolt of weakness thundered through the left half of his body. He crashed to the ground. A stranger, who had seen him lose consciousness, brought him back home. When Daddykins showed up at Doctor's after the incident, his cousin examined him and pronounced him well. A few years afterward, however, a dentist told Daddykins that he noticed a distinct warping on his cheek that suggested that he'd had a mild stroke on his left side. Doctor was mortified about the misdiagnosis. Daddykins learned, too late, that he could not undo the damage of that morning. He would forever be the man with the crooked mouth.

* * *

My father always climbed the stairs to his apartment by holding the banister with his right hand. Following his stay at the hospital, he needed a little help to work his way up. But one day two months after his hospitalisation, I saw him overcome by such weakness that climbing a step proved to be a Herculean task, one before which we had to remove his sandals. He said later that they had felt like pewter beneath his feet. That afternoon, my father had experienced harrowing pain. Daddykins had been at work at his desk when he tried to catch the attention of his colleague before passing out. When Vinayagam called me on the phone, I left our apartment door wide open and ran downstairs. I saw the car turn into our driveway. I opened the door and held a hand out to my father.

He was too weak to take it. He sat inside, unseeing, boneless in appearance, folded over like a wet rag; it seemed to me that he had been in a spin cycle inside the washer. His feet were bare, his pants and shirt patchy with splotches of wetness in several places. I reached out to touch his arm. It was cold.

Vinayagam nudged him gently out of the car, shifting his legs out in slow motion. Daddykins was too weak to will his legs from the car to the floor of the little open garage. Together, the three of us inched towards the first four steps that led us to the short stairwell. My father leaned on Vinayagam, who seemed to bear all his weight on his body. I tucked my father's arm in mine and we carried him up those eighteen steps, six inches at a time, until we saw the light of the day reflected from the Tanjore painting—The Teaching of the Bhagavad Gita—on the wall of Daddykins' living room.

In silence, we helped him out of his clothes. We eased my father onto his bed where he spent the next twenty-four hours in agony.

10

In a Little Crooked House

In the middle of the night, I heard a sound that of a coconut hitting concrete. While aiming for the pillow in the dark, it seems Daddykins' head had hit the headboard of his bed.

I wanted to make sure that nothing had gone wrong. I did the obvious.
'What's 1 + 1, Daddykins?' I asked into the night.
'2,' he said.
'Good job. What's 2 + 2?'
'4.'
'Great. Now what's 1 + 3?'
'7,' Daddykins said. 'You're testing me so now I thought I'd test you instead.'

~ ~ ~

And right when we all thought that Daddykins' health had become so fragile that all our outings of a social nature would have to be folded and put away into our past, he tended to will himself, almost miraculously, back into shape, so he could attend daily concerts in the December festival season. One evening early in the month, my father was ready by 3.15 PM to leave for the inauguration of the music and dance season at Narada Gana Sabha. Vinayagam came up to my room and told me that my father was restless, that he was pacing the floor of the living room like a panther in heat. When I finally appeared in his circle of vision, Daddykins was perched on the edge of the old teak chair. He was sporting a white, full-sleeved shirt over grey dress pants. He looked pointedly at his watch.

'I thought one of the reasons you were in Chennai was also to escort me to a few concerts around town during my convalescence,' he said, adjusting his wristwatch. 'We have two excellent front-row tickets and everyone knows me personally at the sabha.' His eyes were cold. 'And I happen to believe in and expect punctuality.' Then Daddykins got up, turned around and made for the door. His chauffeur gloated behind him.

At the venue, Vinayagam dropped us off at the porch and pick-up area that led directly into the best seats in the house. The staff at the theatre walked up to Daddykins and asked after his health. He introduced me to them. 'My little girl,' he said. Fifty-one years old, with hair dyed black to retain her youth and on supplements to stave off the onset of osteoporosis and peripheral neuropathy, his 'little' girl held Daddykins by the elbow and led him to their seats in the first row.

At every concert, a half-hour into the performance, Daddykins would shrink into the seat, frozen to the bone. Air-conditioning in the theatre could not be regulated, according to the staff. Regulation of any kind in Chennai—of fans, air-conditioning, the size of road pavements, auto fares, the price of lentils—was often the exception, not the norm.

When it got icicle-cold inside the theatre, I draped a woollen shawl that I always carried in my bag around Daddykins' bony torso. The concert would begin. Daddykins listened keenly for the first couple of songs after which he slept through most of the performance; with the loss of hearing, my father seemed unable to recognise the nuances of the music. Although the melodies didn't

seem to nourish his brain anymore, I suspect they were seeping
into his soul through his skin.

* * *

I was embarrassed to be seen with my father. He dropped me off
at Vidyodaya School every morning in his Lambretta scooter. I
knew, even though I was only seven or eight, that though I had
preferred to keep my father's face a secret—to myself, to my family
and my large extended family—it had leaked through the gaps of
the thorny fence of our bungalow.

On and off, I'd see a child distorting the mouth to match that
of my father until the parent, embarrassed and apologetic, dragged
the child away. Sometimes, children asked him why his mouth
was 'like that.' My father would quickly reassure the parent; the
mother's relief was palpable. He'd turn to tell the child that he
had suffered an illness called a 'stroke' and that at the time his
cheek had gravitated to the left and that his mouth too moved
along with it.

The questions didn't last too long because my father flung open
his bag of tricks in the presence of children. First, he hypnotised
them with his butterfly gig. The butterfly needed both a sleight
of all his fingers and an accompanying whistle, as an imaginary
insect soared into the air. For the subsequent trick that I called
'Jack-in-the-box', Daddykins tapped the top of his head and his
tongue snuck out in the centre of his mouth. Next, he tweaked his
right ear; his tongue careened right. Then he tweaked his left ear;
his tongue swung left. Then he pinched the skin by his Adam's
apple; his tongue rolled back in. He had perfected this to an art
over many years, and his sense of comic timing made kids gape and
roar. Within minutes, they were slaves to his pranks, guffawing
and rolling at his feet and begging him to please, please do it again.

Even though my mother, Urmila and I scoffed at his standard
bag of tricks, every time he played a prank, we found ourselves
laughing hard. His relatives longed for an opportunity to visit,

for while my father's repertoire was old, his delivery of lines was refreshing—like a tonic for the soul—accompanied by a bracing whistle, in a two-tone, characteristic of his slyness. Sometimes, we heard a snatch of mimicry, too, or just a whacky point of view wedged into a topical factoid from current affairs or cinema. And there were always new laughs manufactured around his crooked mouth.

My father let it be known to friends and family that he received favours and pity or a combination of both because, in his words, he very likely cut a sorry figure wherever he went, thanks to his crooked mouth. If he had to skewer through red tape anywhere, say, to buy railway tickets and it was known to be impossible to make a reservation at a busy season, he joked that he could wangle a few tickets because, after all, every clerk would take pity on him, a hapless man with a crooked mouth. Daddykins' physical infirmity was a gradual manifestation of a skewed mind that diffused from brain into soul and chin. He attempted to wear his mouth with such panache on his person that he often joked about it as if it belonged below someone else's nose.

11

The Guide

One morning Vinayagam, who was helping Daddykins get dressed, was humming a raga, something he often did, especially around Chennai's music season.

'Saar, seems you don't like me singing?' he asked, buttoning my father's shirt. 'You're not saying anything?'

'I don't want to.'

'Why, Saar?'

'I don't want interrupt the flow,' Daddykins said. 'Just in case something really good should come out of you.'

~ ~ ~

By the following March, Daddykins could not even swallow his pills. Vinayagam powdered all the medication using a stone mortar and pestle and then mixed the powder with water. Grimacing, Daddykins pushed it down his throat. Vinayagam also pureed his food to formlessness. For lunch, the young man cooked rice, vegetable and lentil in the pressure cooker, and ground it to a puree with salt and pepper. For a second course, he blended steamed rice and yoghurt. Daddykins succumbed to the new challenges of old age in a slow, measured way, inching towards the unknown as if by an infinite force, reducing his quantity of food from a plate one month, to a bowl the next, and then to a cup until he couldn't subtract any more.

Jeeva Park kept his mind sharp. I knew just how perceptive he still was on the morning an elderly gentleman reeking of alcohol came on to me. On the very first greeting, the man's eyes flitted around my bosom like a bee on an Indian balsam and so I stiffened when the no-good who introduced himself as Daddykins' walking acquaintance let his hand slide from my shoulder onto my back. I let it pass one time. But when the man was excessively affectionate for a second time during the course of our morning walk, I squirmed. Daddykins flinched. 'I noticed that blackguard's hand on you,' he muttered. 'Uncalled for.'

So, the following morning when the man hung behind us during our walk, Daddykins flanked me on the right where the man couldn't cut in at all. When the lech attempted to greet us both, Daddykins gave him an icy glare. Later, my father told me he couldn't understand how anyone could be inebriated in the morning, a precious time for prayer and contemplation.

He pointed out that he didn't approve of my love of margaritas either. I reminded him about his rule of thumb in life: 'Everything in moderation.' But Daddykins said he didn't believe it was realistic to achieve temperance in alcohol. 'Drinking adulterates one's sense of propriety,' he said. 'To be in complete control, you must shun alcohol.'

***

Daddykins allowed himself the occasional cigarette during our years in the bungalow on Parthasarathypuram Road. As a little girl, I caught the glow of his cigarette when, sometimes, I looked up from the courtyard at our roof terrace. In another way, too, our bungalow's rectangular courtyard made a profound impression on me as a baby of one. I was dropped head down on it, from a height of about three feet, by Urmila. My mother flogged her with a coconut broom for letting my head hit the concrete.

When my father led me into a planetarium in my later life, I was not impressed. It was never that much different from standing in the middle of the courtyard of our bungalow at night, right after dinner, when all of us, my father, my mother, my paternal grandparents, my sister and I relaxed in our verandah with all the lights turned off inside the house. In the dark warm night cooled by the zephyr from the Bay of Bengal under the soft amber of an occasional streetlight, I would hold out my arms and look up, pirouetting, until the heavens swam rapidly over my head and I fell down. The sky shimmered with possibility.

Visiting family loved our cool bungalow, from verandah to backyard, built in accordance with the traditional Hindu principles of good fortune. From the entryway into our home, we saw the *tulsi* plant rising in the middle of the backyard. In such a home, said an astrologer, Goddess Lakshmi would shower wealth, luck and peace. My father remarked that he saw everything in that home—other than money and peace of mind.

We met relatives travelling from the north to the south, or vice versa—since ours were scattered in Delhi, Nagpur, Bombay, Calcutta, Rourkela, Ahmedabad, Cochin, Coimbatore—for they would come home before changing trains at Madras Central Station. Visitors called our home India's other Mughalsarai Junction—a place where people could alight, eat, shower, change, shop, relax, laugh and transfer. Daddykins grumbled that his home was also Bedbug Central, thanks to all the luggage that rolled in and out.

Our dining table was always too small. So the younger ones ate while seated on the cool mosaic floor right by a series of calendars that my father hung by a thread on the wall. One of those yearly calendars was a print of a Ravi Varma painting of a female deity. Another was a glossy calendar from Air India that everyone then coveted as if it were an original lithograph from the Picasso Estate

Collection. My father strung all the calendars on a single twine, taking the trouble to show them off in the dining area.

While many a marriage was brokered in our living room, all too often, it seemed our bungalow was a convalescent home. Madras was famous for its specialist physicians. Thus, Daddykins hovered over relatives with brain tumours, ulcers, gall bladder surgeries, hysterectomies, hernias, hydroceles and urinary complications. Some scenes from my childhood are etched in my brain, especially the vignettes of my uncle Babu.

In the late sixties, Babu suffered a head injury when an auto-rickshaw he was riding in toppled over. For months, he received electric shock therapy—a line of treatment that was shunned in the latter half of the 20th century owing to its side effects—during which time Daddykins and my grandfather would ferry him to his sessions. The threesome returned home in a black and yellow taxi. My grandfather and Daddykins held Babu close between them, his glasses in one of their pockets. They guided him up the three mosaic steps from the courtyard into the verandah and then into the living room, turning right into the bedroom where a little mattress and pillow lay on the cool floor ready to welcome my uncle. He slept for hours, until the effects of the therapy wore off. He recovered from his trauma and went on to marry and have a beautiful family of his own. Our bungalow really did seem to swallow a passel of bad and spit out plenty of good.

Like most homes of that period, ours too was cleaved in the typical mode of the day, a clear line demarcating the duties of my father and those of my mother at a time when women slogged in the home while men went to work. Daddykins was considerate to my mother in a Brahmin culture that upheld male chauvinism as a virtue. But every other day, he let it be known—in his wife's earshot—that she couldn't bear to see him sitting idly in our verandah. Whenever he sat down to read *The Hindu* after his morning coffee, his wife had to thrust another errand on him that had to be done right that second. She was demanding even after all her demands were met. For instance, every time Daddykins trudged back home from the vegetable market, my mother would empty the bags and wonder about the one item that he had not bought. 'You didn't buy drumstick?' she would say with a petulant curl of her lip. 'Now how do I make *avial* without drumstick? Just go back and get it!' Daddykins protested. 'Why can't you make do with whatever I've bought?' he asked. She retorted that his meal and his coffee would suffer greatly if Daddykins cramped her style. Cursing, Daddykins would rumble down the road again in his scooter to buy her drumsticks after informing her that she was peevish.

One time, my mother remained inconsolable. She had been ailing from a dreadful fluid collection resulting from mosquito bites that she feared might render her leg forever gigantic as an elephant's foot. Daddykins and my mother were en route to Doctor's to get her condition diagnosed when Daddykins pressed the brake of his Lambretta much too hard upon seeing a cow in his path. My mother tumbled onto the road. My father vroomed off, oblivious.

Later, when they returned home, my mother's face was purple. She wept. She had fallen on the road in a most disgraceful manner. How could he have driven off? This dragged them both over a land mine. Any suggestion of her corpulence made her angrier still for while she was a woman of considerable proportions, she didn't like to be reminded of it and asking why Daddykins could not have sensed that the vehicle was lighter was a direct admission of guilt about her impressive girth. Never again would my mother grace his scooter with the weight of her glance or the heft of her seat.

* * *

'Like most of the men of his era, Daddykins used to smoke at least one cigarette a day for many years,' I said to Vinayagam. But I wanted to verify with my father whether it was one or two or more. Daddykins, who was seated in his leather chair in the living room, did not respond. But he looked sideways and told me, in Queen's English, that he was irked that I would have sought to bring it up for discussion at that moment, and that too when we were surrounded by a good-for-nothing like 'this fellow' by which he obviously meant Vinayagam, who, in his opinion, tended to blow everything out of proportion.

'*Saar!*' Vinayagam cried, barely able to contain his mirth and not caring a fig for the insult levelled at him in English by his boss. 'You too were wild once, *Saar*.' He stood behind Daddykins caressing his baldpate. 'In any case, *Saar*, how many?'

I jumped in. 'One or two cigarettes a day, that's all, for many years. Maybe one at work too, every day?' Daddykins looked straight ahead into the black hole of our television. Vinayagam cackled while I elaborated upon it. 'When we built the portion of our bungalow upstairs in 1970, he'd go up after dinner to hide and smoke. Until, one day, just like that, he dropped the habit. Isn't that right, Daddykins?'

As if in response to my question, my father picked up the remote to the television and pressed it several times, forcibly, while sending austere glances in my direction, murderous looks that informed me that I was thoughtless and irreverent to have brought up such a discussion in front of a certain rascal whose only business it would be to tom-tom it to the rest of the world in flagrant disregard of a man's age and station in life. Vinayagam yanked the remote from Daddykins's hand and increased the volume.

My father leaned back in his chair. His favourite anchor, Barkha Dutt, was on NDTV along with five prominent panelists. In a few minutes, Daddykins' irritation over the cigarette discussion quelled, he now began simmering over the mishandling of the Delhi gang rape case. He told me he prayed that the trial of the six accused rapists would move quickly to the date of execution. 'Those men need to be hanged now. I really do not see a need for a trial!' A man who wouldn't crush a cockroach now favoured capital punishment. I believe my father often felt a physical pain as he watched the country of his birth putrefy. Seated in front of his Sony Bravia, Daddykins was now wondering aloud whether the prime minister of India had a cock.

12

Cary Grant of Parthasarathypuram

Daddykins would not listen when Samyuktha, his youngest sibling by a whole twenty-three years, told him that he need not attend a famous singing duo's four-hour concert at Tapovan Hall.

'Haven't you heard them perform often enough?' Samyuktha asked. 'I say there's no need for you to go!'

'So what if I heard them a few months ago?' Daddykins retorted, grimmer than a coconut tree in the Tundra. 'Don't you eat every day?'

~ ~ ~

Thalaivar rarely arrived at Daddykins' apartment unannounced, calling ahead to ensure no visitors were home, preferring to talk to his father-in-law in private. The telephone call was a sign for Vinayagam to turn on the air-conditioner so the room would be cool upon his arrival.

In early February, I had called Thalaivar in Singapore to convey my father's anxiety about maintaining a retinue of household staff as his illness progressed. I felt Thalaivar would be able to stanch his insecurities and a week after our chat, Thalaivar landed in Chennai.

The morning of Thalaivar's phone call, Vinayagam rushed into the living room to turn on the air-conditioner. Then he scampered into Daddykins' bedroom to fetch his hearing aid so that they could both avoid receiving a lecture from Thalaivar on why Daddykins must always wear the earpieces from dawn until bedtime.

Thalaivar strode in at the appointed time, dressed to kill, as always. A sharp trail of expensive perfume now clung to the living room. Daddykins awaited his son-in-law in the farthest corner of the room, right by the television, away from the cold blast.

Years before, Urmila and Thalaivar had installed air-conditioners in several rooms in my father's apartment to ensure that my parents were comfortable in their old age in Chennai's mercury-melting heat. But Daddykins never turned it on saying it didn't suit his chest. I knew it didn't agree with his wallet.

On the day of his visit, my brother-in-law got to the point after dispensing with basic niceties. His manner often verged on the brusque. 'Don't imagine that Vinayagam takes care of you simply because you are special to him,' he said. 'You may well be, but please know that his future is secure. I am taking care of him too. And I'll take good care of him even after you are gone.' Daddykins leaned forward and patted him on the arm. 'I know you will. Thank you.' Thalaivar looked at Daddykins with the intensity typical of him when he was having a one-on-one conversation. 'I want you to know that more than his monthly salary and all the little things that you or I have bought him, you have taught Vinayagam a lot of things that will stay with that fellow through his life. You cannot put a price on that.' He touched my father's wrist. 'You have taught Vinayagam to manage his money. You have taught him to be meticulous. You have taught him discipline. You have taught him diligence. You have taught him to believe in the divine. You have taught him so much about life. Do you know what those things mean to a man like him—to someone who came to you when he was a boy of eighteen—when he was a nobody?'

My father wiped the ends of his eyes with the edge of his dhoti. I know he had not heard his somewhat dry son-in-law address him like that before. Thalaivar laughed softly and he looked at Daddykins for a time. His demeanour switched back to his business-like self. 'You know, your problem is that you look at life as checks and balances. You keep accounts of everything. You go by the book.'

I caught Daddykins stealing a glance at the clock.

'Do you know that I've never worried about who will take care of me in the future?'

'Really?' Daddykins asked, startled. 'Why not?'

'I'm taking care of many people now, especially those in my employ,' Thalaivar said, 'and so I believe that there is a supreme power up above that I can trust implicitly to take care of me when I'm old and infirm and I need help.'

Daddykins gasped out loud. I sensed both awe and incredulity in my father's reaction. I doubt he was convinced that such an assumption on Thalaivar's part was safe in the long term.

I too believed in karma in my present life, like Thalaivar. He was generous. In turn, of course, he expected loyalty, especially from his staff. Whenever Thalaivar was about to leave our home, the help in our house stood around, a trifle sheepishly, out of respect for the big boss. Thalaivar then slipped a finger into his pocket and fished out a crisp bill with the soundless grace of a cheetah, and pressed the tip into the helper's palm. Though he never referred to it, Thalaivar had educated several disadvantaged children through the years. Long after Thalaivar left our apartment that evening, I sat in the lingering cloud of Hugo Boss. I had been allowed a peek into his soul, if only for a fraction of a second.

* * *

My father's Lambretta roared into the romance between Thalaivar and my sister. Over time, Daddykins' two wheels staked out the venues of their clandestine meetings. As the young sweethearts got bolder, Thalaivar would await my sister in his clunky Ambassador car at the bus stop at the intersection of Habibullah Road and North Usman Road. On occasion, Daddykins waited at the stop, along with my sister, just to make sure she boarded the city bus to college. But sometimes, before he knew what was happening, she would slip away into the waiting Ambassador and Daddykins would just watch in utter disbelief, jaw dropping, before turning around to go back home.

My parents were aghast that in an era of arranged marriages, their child would choose the man she wished to marry. Daddykins may also have been concerned that his daughter's name was linked with a boy who seemed to be a Casanova in a neighbourhood of stodgy Tamil Brahmins. Thalaivar wore loud shirts. He walked with a swagger that suggested that he might own Parthasarathypuram Road one day.

However, this Cary Grant of Parthasarathypuram impressed a betel-chewing college principal and another math professor, both of whom lived across our bungalow. They told Daddykins that he needed to have a better reason to prevent him from marrying his daughter. Thalaivar was an academic star from a decent family. He had degrees in physics and electronics. His job prospects were excellent. Just what more did a father want for his daughter, they asked.

Thalaivar lived in the bungalow diagonally across from our backyard. For the longest time, a short barbed wire ran throughout the perimeter of our bungalow to deter burglars. The first thing my father did when he came into more money in the late sixties was to erect a brick wall in place of the barbed wire that separated us from passers-by. It's possible that Daddykins just wanted to prevent unwanted romance.

On some days, while walking past our house and almost always when our parents were out of the house, Thalaivar bounded across our courtyard, entered our verandah and slipped a book to me through the window to be handed over to my sister. For a time, I thought that an exchange of books happened between a man and a woman when they were intellectually engaged. But I missed the other exchange—the exchange of looks. At a time when almost no one we knew owned a telephone in their home, I had become the clueless go-between of neighbourhood sweethearts.

At five or six, I hadn't yet worked out human cunning but looking back at it all now, I remember dropping my full ice cream cup on a day the ice cream man rode into our street. Thalaivar ran across the road to pacify me with a new one even though my parents felt no such compulsion.

Thalaivar summoned every resource into his courtship. I suppose my brother-in-law's goal-oriented approach in business was tested first in his acquisition of a wife of his choice. He also roped in one of his sisters for a business partner. The oldest of the girls in the family, she became my sister's confidante. She invited her for family outings. Without knowing what was happening right under his reading glasses, my father was aiding and abetting a romance at a time when courtship was objectionable.

The road separating our home from Thalaivar's bubbled over with the Hindi and Tamil melodies of the late sixties: *Mere sapnon ki rani kab aayegi tu; Jeena yahan marna yahan, Iske siwa jaana kahan; Aaayiram nilavey vaa*. While Thalaivar stood in the open terrace leading out of his room, the lyrics from his blaring radio upstairs filled the road as he looked diagonally across into our backyard where his heroine stood strategically, for way longer than necessary, combing her luxuriant tresses, reminding him, perhaps, of the doe-eyed glamour queen of Bollywood, Asha Parekh.

For those of us who blossomed into adolescence in the late sixties, nothing rivalled the innocent romance of the Bollywood screen—even though Bollywood borrowed heavily from Hollywood, imitating the plastic roses, the ribbons, the bows, the white gloves, the cat-eyes and the bullet bras. Everyone then was in love with the idea of being in love. Thalaivar and Urmila were the little stars in my firmament, a young couple of twenty-three and twenty-two, whose marriage immortalised the notion that all love—not just the one seen on the silver screen—had a fairy-tale ending.

In a dramatic turn of events that was evocative of all the Hindi and Tamil movies that Thalaivar himself loved to watch, the debonair hero in my sister's life suffered an acute attack of typhoid during which he extracted a promise from his mother that she would get him married to Urmila if he recovered.

In June 1972, my sister was formally engaged to be married to Thalaivar and their wedding in September, at Hemamalini Kalyana Mandapam, was an opulent affair even though, it was orchestrated by an ordinary man who, by his own constant admission, was nothing more than an inconsequential bean counter working for the government of India.

* * *

My father's pants had begun flapping around his limbs like laundry on the drying lines. His rate of atrophy was alarming. The evening before Thalaivar flew back to Singapore at the end of January, he called Daddykins at home to tell him they were going shopping for clothes.

Thalaivar had decided that his father-in-law also needed a luxurious leather chair—one at home for watching television and a more comfortable leather chaise-longue for work in the office— on which he could stretch out and rest. He ferried Daddykins and Vinayagam to two furniture stores before arriving at Raymonds at Pondy Bazaar where they didn't find pants in Daddykins' size. My father was so slight that the store suggested looking in a shop for boys. They went to Mahaveer a few doors away where they found pants in a size that would work, with some alteration.

Halfway through this outing, Daddykins was exhausted. Vinayagam tried to call this, in vain, to Thalaivar's attention.

By the time Thalaivar dropped off Daddykins at 9 PM, at least three hours after the mission began, my father was winded, hungry and crabby, and sporting a brand new shirt in sky blue, fitting his shrunken frame to perfection.

In Vinayagam's hand was a booty: four new pants, six new shirts and two swanky sandals, a closed shoe with a buckle that would be light on Daddykins feet, especially as he climbed the stairs to his house, and another light, open pair, for casual wear. A leather recliner would be arriving the following morning.

My father was sour. 'The man gets something into his head that has to be done now and we all have to follow his orders.'

I sat down by my father's side. 'Don't crib, Daddykins,' I said, hugging his frail body. He proceeded to sulk. He felt cold to the touch. I told him his son-in-law wanted him to look good and feel good. 'He bought you pants for 2500 rupees a pop. Whoever does that?' Apparently, no one inside the car had cared that an old man could not take the blast of air-conditioning. 'But there's a limit, I'm almost ninety,' he said.

Vinayagam looked exhausted too. He had tried telling Thalaivar that Daddykins' energy flagged by early evening. But he had been too nervous to press the case. 'Amma, you don't understand. Thalaivar talks. We never talk. Especially not underlings like me.'

I insisted that Thalaivar was not unreasonable and that he should have been more forceful. But Vinayagam shook his head. 'Amma, there was no way to get through.'

Daddykins sat down to eat. He spooned his dinner into his mouth in stony silence. At the table, Vinayagam opened Daddykins' pillbox and picked out the capsules.

'Thalaivar didn't intend to do so many things, Amma. You know how he is. He's a perfectionist. He believes in finishing everything that he thinks of right at that given minute. He doesn't postpone anything.'

I looked at Daddykins. Now that his stomach was a little full, he seemed to have become more composed. Vinayagam set the stone mortar and pestle on the table and turned to me.

'Amma, in your story you must say that when your father became too skinny and began looking like a scarecrow in a sugarcane field, his son-in-law decided to take him shopping one evening.'

While Daddykins continued to slurp the white puree of curd and rice seasoned with salt, Vinayagam began pounding the pills, one by one, in the stone mortar. He looked up and pointed the pestle in my direction.

'And you must say also that your father is too miserly and too old-world and too principled to spend money on himself. And that he still calls himself a penniless clerk, even after all these years. All that should appear in your book, Amma, for your story to be honest.' He stopped to glare at me, brow raised, as if he had just had another epochal realisation. 'At this rate, I think I might as well write the book for you, Amma.'

13

Really Broke

Daddykins griped that his wife didn't ever walk at Jeeva Park. The few times that my mother strolled in the park under hardship and duress, she began her walk with a pleasant enough face but always returned home with a glower. She even went about making herself a pair of leather sandals for the purposes of her walk—snug ones with a strap and buckle—at Mylapore's National Leather Works. But she made excuses about heat, or wind, or sun, or noise, or dust, or sweat, or cold, or rain.

One evening, while he was pottering about the house after work, Daddykins' eyes happened to fall on my mother's leather sandals. He turned to his valet in the presence of his wife.

'Vinayagam, do you know what kind of sandals these are?' His chauffeur shook his head.

'These, young man, are the kind that never go walking.'

~ ~ ~

As we approached Jeeva Park in the morning, Daddykins stopped at his usual spot, where Sambasivam Street met our street. Hands folded in prayer, my father looked to the left where a Ganesha stared out of a sconce in the wall. He sought the blessings of the deity behind the bars inside the alcove. Then he looked to the right to seek the blessings of the Ganesha idol at the far end on Raghavaiah Road.

I touched his arm as he paid obeisance to the deities. 'What do you ask of your god every morning?' I asked, guiding him past potholes that got filled up by the road workers every few months only to cave in with the next downpour.

'Peace of mind,' my father said. 'You can have everything in the world. But it isn't always easy to have peace of mind.' I had heard my father use the term a lot around our house. As a child, I'd thought it was something like milk or sugar, kept in the larder perhaps.

As we reached the park, I told Daddykins to watch out for the thin, black pipe that had surfaced again, out of the mud, for the nth time in weeks. We began with my father stepping onto the track to announce, as he did every day, that he felt better than usual. After a few minutes on the track, Daddykins ran into his two walking friends at which point he told me that I was free to walk on my own.

As I wandered away, a Carnatic aria floated in from the speakers and I thought about how for years my father had sought peace of mind in classical music. When Daddykins was composed, we heard it in his whistles, in his jokes, and in his daily banter. However, my father succumbed to stress and morphed into his antipode on at least one day in a month.

On the days leading up to that unfortunate moment, my father would tell my mother that she or someone else was draining his peace of mind. He'd then spend twenty hours in agony, cotton cloth wound tightly around his head, thrashing about in bed in a migraine that siphoned him off into an alien world of turbid and one-sided pain, nausea, vomiting, and sensitivity to light.

Daddykins suffered many such migraines in the months leading to the milestone event of our family—Urmila's wedding to Thalaivar. The wedding robbed my father of all peace of mind even though, in 1972, when he finally got over his disapproval of his daughter falling in love, he felt that her marriage to a smart young banker was the highest point of his life. Unfortunately, his happiness was marred by his realisation that it would also spell the lowest point in his bank balance.

For a man who took stock of everyone's spending every night, the first wedding in his own family was bound to come as something of a shock to his system. When he opened his black accounts diary, he became fearful that everything he had worked for would vanish overnight. It would dissolve at the pillars of ostentation erected by the women of his house. This was, after all, a man who lived with two pens, four sets of underwear and six shirts and three pairs of trousers.

He drew up a plan of expenditure. He informed my mother and Urmila that they had to stay inside the circle he had drawn for them. He allotted my sister 2000 rupees for her trousseau from which she would have to buy a total of five Kanchipuram silk sarees. My sister was concerned that the amount he had assigned for her purchase was inadequate for what she wanted: at least two grand silk saris. My father suggested that perhaps she could buy one grand sari, and four ordinary saris. Thus, one of her saris had an imitation gold border and not real silver thread coated in pure gold, a sartorial choice many brides would have balked at in the 70s.

Daddykins also wished to make it clear to Thalaivar's parents that they needed to temper their expectations of how he would conduct the wedding because his coffers were not immeasurably deep. Daddykins walked up to their house one morning, eight weeks before the date of the wedding to request their understanding.

'Sir, you are a jeweller, a diamond merchant,' my father said to Thalaivar's father. 'If you have to spend a little extra on something, all you may have to do is take another purchase order and you'll make the money you spent right away. The business world gives you the flexibility to make a little profit to adjust if you must. But in my line of work—remember that I'm only an indigent servant of the government of India—even if I were to work another ten hours a week, my salary would stay stagnant.' Thalaivar's father listened politely. A polished, soft-spoken gentleman with a comforting way about him, he assured Daddykins that he would have nothing at all to worry about.

Daddykins' anxiety did not abate. Soon, however, he was swept away by the feverish excitement of a wedding in his home. A week before the big day, adirasam—sweetened browned discs of flour, cane sugar and cardamom—began frying in the makeshift shed in the back of our bungalow. Relatives hadn't seen that size of adirasam. Murukkus aligned themselves in biscuit tins to be ferried across to the home of the groom. Chickpea flour shuddered through sieves and was roasted in iron woks as wide as the Aracibo. Laddoos rolled into steel plates. Cooks whipped up meals and snacks and the bungalow buzzed with the laughter of relatives who arrived from both sides of the family for several days. By night, the men in the home carted their pillows and grass mats to the verandah and slept there, even as mosquitoes buzzed about in the humid September sky.

Henna trees rambled along one side of our home all the way to the well in the back. Our maid picked leaves by the bucketfuls. She crushed them in my mother's stone grinder in batches, making a tight, smooth paste. My aunts lined Urmila's hands and feet with henna, like those of a dancer, making a thick coat all around the periphery. They capped each of her toes and her fingers so the dye coloured the nails and painted them a bright rust. My cousins and I painted our hands and feet, too, and when we grew impatient of waiting for it to dry, we hobbled to the tap by the well and washed our hands and feet, rubbing until the dried henna washed off. A rust-orange emerged. We took our hands to our noses and breathed deep the smell of leaf, soil and sun.

Days before the two-day wedding, a truckload of produce arrived by car from the town of Pollachi. Groceries arrived from the local Bombay Stores. At the end of the festivities of the first evening, Daddykins was caught totally off guard. The kitchen staff ran out of all produce and all other groceries; in exactly one evening, the cooks had exhausted everything planned for the three-event wedding. Panic ensued. At midnight, Daddykins' siblings knocked on the door of the grocer to buy fresh supplies for the morning's events.

My father needed cash overnight for the unexpected expenditure. He called the only person who would have that kind of cash under his pillow: Doctor. Daddykins accepted the loan of 9000 rupees with the tacit agreement to repay it over the next many years at zero interest.

When everyone had left for their respective hometowns after the wedding, life did not assume normalcy. I would stand in the last room of our home, on our concrete floor, looking through the grill at Thalaivar's home, desperate for a glimpse of my sister. Her growing roots in another home felt like an abandonment of our own. In the meantime, Daddykins brooded over his new circumstances. He had been toying with the idea of working abroad. The stack of wedding bills firmed up his resolve. He accepted an offer to work as an auditor with the Tanzanian government in Dar-es-Salaam.

In December, Daddykins, my mother and I flew to a life in East Africa. Some of his siblings felt my father was shirking his duty as the first child and the first son to his aged parents. But it was a risk he had to take. Daddykins was stone-broke.

***

After his walk one morning, Daddykins stood grumbling behind the open door of his almirah. 'I'm paying that bloody fellow so he will take me to where I bloody well want to go,' Daddykins said. 'That's his bloody job.'

I found out that when Vinayagam had arrived that morning, his boss had greeted him at the door saying that he wanted to go to the bank. But whenever Vinayagam heard the words 'the bank,' his face assumed the aura of a bank vault—gray, steely, impenetrable. He hated taking Daddykins to the bank.

On the first of every month, Daddykins worried about all the payments that needed to be made. He worried about his income—work, dividends, pension—tiding him over for all the expenses that he would incur for the month. He would then go to the bank, check on his accounts and ensure that an entry, in pen, was made in his accounts passbook.

Little had changed inside the bank since the time it had opened in T. Nagar in the seventies. The building had hardly been updated. There was nowhere to park nearby. Vinayagam had rightly noted that Daddykins' perception of levels was so poor that he would be unsafe if left to make his way on his own inside the bank in spite of my father insisting that Vinayagam was exaggerating.

Vinayagam's monthly ire wasn't at the trip itself, it was at the monthly insult of Daddykins not just letting Vinayagam do it alone. Everyone inside the bank had known Vinayagam for two decades. Daddykins could just give him the passbook, the check, the letter and Vinayagam would zip down in his two-wheeler, have any and all the work done and bring the passbook back, all neat and stamped.

Daddykins said, however, that he wished to be seen. And that he wished to oversee his own affairs. As long as blood purled through his veins, and as long as his two legs would ferry him to a destination and back, he would go to the bank himself, he declared.

The morning in question, all three of us made the trip. Vinayagam stopped right outside the entrance and I gave Daddykins a hand and led him in after warning him about the thick electric cables that snaked outside the pathway and crept into a hole in the wall that acted like an electrical junction.

'Do you realise just how dangerous this is?' I asked Daddykins. 'Vinayagam was right. You cannot walk in here without an escort.' Daddykins scowled.

I told my father to sit down in the waiting area, while I took his accounts passbook to the female officer, who would make an entry in the book and arrange for a withdrawal of 9000 rupees for his expenses—in hundred, twenty rupee bills—with the rest in hundreds and thousands. But Daddykins made a beeline to her desk, bantered with her, asked after her family and introduced me as his little girl from California.

Then, while my father sat, I took his passbook to the teller's counter. I began waiting in a line that that ran straight across, like a chorus of Can-Can dancers in front of the man's desk. The teller asked who was first in the queue, such as it was. Everyone extended their passbooks. Twenty minutes later, the gentleman handed over my father's money to me. The bills tucked away in his black leather wallet, my father, Vinayagam and I headed home.

Home and eased into his teak chair, Daddykins began—'That teller at the bank was such a slowcoach today,' he said with a smile, extending a foot forward so his man Friday could unbuckle his shoe. Vinayagam told his boss that he was an uncharitable one. To label others as 'slow' when he himself moved slower than a snail? 'How was that fair, *Saar*?' he asked. And Daddykins, who couldn't let that go uncontested, told him that it was one thing to be slow at the age of ninety and quite another thing to be wooden-headed when you were a strapping young lad of thirty.

Vinayagam snorted. Upon seeing the effect of his rejoinder on Vinayagam, Daddykins chortled into his right palm, as he always did, when he realised he had been an old hooligan.

Everyone was happy again. For a time at least, there would be peace of mind.

14

The Bwana in a Safari Suit

One morning, just as we were about to head out for our walk in Jeeva Park, I noticed that Daddykins had worn his walking shorts inside out. The pockets flapped about like the ears of a pet dachshund.

When I brought it to his attention, he looked down in annoyance. 'No wonder I couldn't find my pockets,' he said, cursing into the air because he had already worn his walking shoes and tied his laces and tucked them inside his shoes.

And then while he sat in the teak chair in his Crystal tighty-whities, I tore off his shorts and turned them inside out and slid them past his shoes again. He pulled them up his knees and thanked me, apologising for having embarrassed me by asking me to help him with mishaps of an intimate nature.

~~~

The first time Juma, our housekeeper in Dar-es-Salaam, winked at me, I was eleven years old. I had no idea until then that men tried to endear themselves to girls.

Juma was harmless, but that wink was the first of many jolts about my changing body. Prior to this, I had figured out something about sex from the Hindi movie *Aradhana*, gleaning that if a man and a woman were lying next to each other by the fireplace and they were attractive, things could happen right when the Hindi song came alive through the speakers.

Roop Tera Mastana
Pyar Mera Diwana
Bhool Koi Hamse Naa
Ho Jaaye

A cousin explained the meaning of the lyrics to me. She said that the male was so intoxicated by the female that something could happen between them that would be a very grave mistake indeed.

I spent many years in Dar trying to figure out what that something was. The research happened as I developed. I was helped further along by 'uncles' and other family friends, whose glances made me feel uncomfortable and so I began to avoid them. Avoidance marks the end of innocence, I suppose.

The greatest predator was Mr. Mistry in the flat downstairs. He spent his time trying to rope teenage girls in our building into massaging his legs and thighs. If he felt he could get away with it—and predators have an amazing knack for choosing victims—he would ask them to massage other parts of him too. I was spared that trauma, but I fell into the clutches of Kumar, the son of one of Daddykins' friends who was a few years older than me, who tried to feel my breasts whenever our families met up.

At the time, I didn't know how I should tell my mother or Daddykins that I was afraid of this boy. But the night Kumar tried to put his hands between my legs in his Renault while his father was giving our family a ride home, was the day the young man learned to never ever touch me again. I pinched him, twisting his fingers so hard that my nails must have drawn blood. That was also the day I learned that it was important for a woman to kick and fight back even if she couldn't scream.

Many years later, long after we were back in India, I told Daddykins about how in Dar, I had lived as a voiceless victim, like many girls my age, in fear of being groped and torn by feelings of guilt when I didn't even understand the significance or the consequences. Daddykins was apoplectic. He said he wished I'd told him then about what had happened and that he would have guaranteed my safety had he only known.

While I was peeling the layers of my womanhood in Tanzania, my parents were also learning to live a little. For the first time ever they found themselves in their own bubble, experiencing a life they'd not imagined before outside their rigid socio-economic strata and the constant reach of relatives. After years of financial hardship, they felt they had some respite.

We also became more aware of the things money could buy. Daddykins regretted that he could not send his father more than 300 shillings, a third of his salary, every month. Suddenly, he seemed resentful about staying in a job in the government when employees in the private sectors afforded more. Their homes were visibly better. I too saw the difference in the woodwork, the finish of the Danish-style furniture they owned, whereas ours were coarse hand-me-downs, bought second-hand from others, who were leaving town. Some families also had full-time household help. One gentleman in the United Nations pocketed twelve times the salary Daddykins made and did not pay taxes. He was given a car for personal use. His car, the latest Toyota, was soundless. Ours sounded like a sum of all its moving parts.

The flip side of it was that our family had never imagined that one day we would own a car. Weeks after we arrived in Dar, my father realised that it would be difficult to go about his life without his own set of wheels. He saved six months of Tanzanian shillings before he bought his first car.

In June 1973, a light blue sedan, a Vauxhall Viva with four seats—a bucket seat next to driver's seat and two in the back—rolled into our building with Daddykins, sporting a grey safari suit, at the wheel. It cost my father 4000 shillings. There was no excitement greater than the arrival, into our home, of that secondhand car, basic box on four wheels, a not particularly handsome one. But it was a sign to us and to all the relatives back home in India, by means of photographs, that we had arrived. The thing that often brings us the most joy is the awareness that someone else is observing our enjoyment.

I'd lived in a small, conservative town before moving to Dar where, suddenly, I discovered so much, not just about myself but also about the world outside. As I observed life in Dar and the ways of local Tanzanians, I learned that independence didn't always translate to freedom. The locals were a gullible, pious lot trodden upon by centuries of imperialists—first Arabs, then Europeans and finally, in the 20th century, business-minded Indians—who viewed them through selfish, greedy eyes. Daddykins observed that all around the world, the colonised invariably became colonialists. The side we were on depended on how history had treated us.

Poor natives like Juma, with his frizzy hair packed tightly around his head and his eyes spreading like melting butter over his ebony face, were simply trying to climb out of the well of their oppression. I'll forever remember Juma standing outside the ramshackle servants' quarters, rocking to *That's The Way I Like It* by KC & The Sunshine Band, the radio's shiny steel antenna catching the last rays of the evening sun.

***

When I flew back to Chennai from the San Francisco Bay area in the summer of 2013, my companion on the colourless flight was *My Days*, R. K. Narayan's analysis of his own life—an objective and often hilarious assessment of his disappointments, his failures and his accomplishments.

Narayan's struggles as a writer could have been the story of any writer in any decade. The reaction of family and friends to the penury that accompanied the journey of a writer in the 1920s resonated with me almost a whole century later. *My Days* connected with me in other ways too. In a poignant way, the book fused south India, the home of my birth, with the San Francisco Bay Area, the home of my growth. In 1956, Narayan spent several months holed up in an apartment in the city of Berkeley writing *The Guide*, his most memorable work of fiction, right by the Campanile under whose shadow my son now pursued his undergraduate degree. Narayan had been seventeen years older than my father and had risked everything he had to chase his dream.

I bought a large print version of his book for my father and he began reading two pages a day every afternoon after coffee. And even though, sometimes, he found sentences sliding off the page, as if a puppeteer were dragging each line away with a string, and therefore had to read a sentence several times to elicit the literal and the contextual meaning, my father did, in fact, finish the book by the time I returned to the United States in mid-September.

On one of those evenings while he was reading, he stopped to tell me how, in Tanzania, he did not pass an exam that would have fetched him both a promotion and a salary hike. A couple of his friends did, however. 'But what I lacked in ability I made up for with my attitude. What helped me most was my diligence and my perseverance,' he said. 'I was confident and I worked hard, and thus I got an extension to serve another three years in the Tanzanian government.' With the extra money Daddykins made in Dar, he paid off the loan from Doctor and celebrated my wedding without feeling the pinch. I believe my father recognised R. K. Narayan's optimism, good humour and positive spirit in himself.

I would read him passages from other books, too. He listened keenly to Gurcharan Das' *India Unbound*, interrupting me to observe that Das was right or wrong or presumptuous or diplomatic—as if Das had given him the book in manuscript form to critique it. Sometimes, in the middle of it, he would apologise and tell me to stop and reread a section because his mind had drifted. At times, as Das detailed the circumstances of India's independence, my father teared up. The people of his generation would never forget their fight for self-rule, he said. Daddykins had participated in a civil disobedience movement while at Victoria College, skipping classes for a day. But his college principal, Cambridge-educated S. R. U. Savoor, reported to a white man in the Madras Presidency and so, the following day, tail between their legs, Daddykins and his cohorts trooped back through the gates of their college.

When I read out Jawaharlal Nehru's speech broadcast on the day of India's independence, my father mouthed the words along with me, his voice thick with emotion, his face wrenched in nostalgia. 'Long ago we made a tryst with destiny, and now the time comes when we shall redeem our pledge, not wholly or in full measure, but very substantially. At the stroke of the midnight hour, when the world sleeps, India will awake to life and freedom.'

My father removed his glasses. He wiped his tears with the edge of his dhoti.

15

Hakuna Matata

Daddykins always observed how Tanzanians were inherently carefree, shrugging off misfortune with a 'hakuna matata'-no worries, in Swahili—or a 'bahati mbaya'-bad luck—and believing that another day would come and that money would come with the new day.

~~~

Such is the nature of illness that soon Daddykins talked about his esophageal dilation as if it were a condition requiring regular service, like a tyre replacement, an oil change, or a battery check. He would hound us until Urmila or I—whoever had flown down at the time—would call the doctor for a consultation and a procedure. By mid-year, Daddykins could not even eat a puree of steamed idlis with sugar and yoghurt. The stricture was so severe that at its most acute an endoscopy and dilation brought him relief for a few more weeks. We had fallen into a cyclical pattern of blockage and intervention. Vinayagam diluted the purees further. Now, on many afternoons, Daddykins could not swallow his biscuits with his evening coffee.

'But they are the only thing that I can still relish by chewing,' Daddykins said to Vinayagam one afternoon, when he suggested it might be time to stop them. My father flung his newspaper down on the coffee table. It landed in a crackling heap, its crease awry. 'I should have just had that surgery in the first place last August.'

Vinayagam who had been reading *Dina Thandhi* set his paper down on the floor. '*Saar*, you don't understand,' he said, walking over and picking up Daddykins' paper and folding it at its crease. 'If you had elected to have surgery on your digestive tract instead of having a stent put in, you would have gone upstairs a whole year ago.'

While Daddykins continued to sulk into space, Vinayagam carried on in his somewhat tactless fashion. 'In which case we'd be celebrating, right now as we speak, your first year in heaven away from us.' I glared at him.

My father turned to Vinayagam now. 'Fine, take those biscuits away from me too.' He pointed to me and then to Vinayagam. 'All this speculation that you both do. I hate what you and this fellow say. 'Look, it's getting stuck. It's because you ate this. Or you ate that.' I'm tired of your accusations. Sick, sick to death, of your theories!' He sat in his rust-orange sofa, indignant and churlish, until, a few minutes later, he picked up his newspaper.

Despite Vinayagam's manner, his persistence saw us through many challenging meal times. On one such morning, Daddykins had taken barely four spoonfuls of soup when he felt the puree wasn't descending as it should. Water didn't help either. He looked at the two of us and fed himself from the tip of a spoon. That morning, Vinayagam found a way to get Daddykins to finish his food while standing by his side—teasing, laughing, threatening, goading, cajoling and relating gory news stories to entertain him while he ate.

'The problem is you and your sister let him go. I don't,' he said, describing Daddykins' escalating problems in layman's terms. 'He just cannot afford any more endoscopies.' Vinayagam moved back and forth between the dining area and the kitchen busying himself with my lunch, while Daddykins paused to drink hot water. Between sips, Daddykins also stood up and paced the room so the liquid would be forced to drain into his stomach.

'Remember that his throat pipe is like the plastic tubing under our sink, Amma. How many times can I take out that plastic attachment and blow air into it and clean it? Every time I force it and expand it, it will tighten all over again. I assure you there will come a day when we will not be able to do anything about it.'

'Amma, because you have money and we have all this comfort of the car, we have been going to Apollo Hospitals to try to get a procedure to dilate his throat pipe. You know what we would have done in homes like mine and Saravanan's? We would have just brought the person home and resigned ourselves to the fate that the throat pipe had become too constricted to allow anything to pass through. We would have put the person on a milk diet. The person would have steadily lost weight. Because of that, there would likely have been other complications too. After three or four months, the person would have become too weak to move. He would have passed away. And we would have accepted that too.'

Our plumbing guru was right. When my mother's cancer fanned out into her brain, the doctors informed us that radiation of the brain was an option but that the quality of life, or whatever remained of it, would deteriorate rapidly. A better alternative was to halt all treatment, take her home and let her go gently. At the time, Urmila and I had heard our father say that he wanted to do everything within his means to keep her alive. We had the money. We had the help. We had the privileged access to a team of doctors. My mother underwent radiation therapy for a few weeks. Her face changed. She stopped speaking altogether. We had zapped her brain into immediate inaction because we'd had the resources to do so. Money could buy comfort for our family but it failed to guarantee even a modicum of health for our mother.

We were adopting the same route with Daddykins. With every procedure we attempted to buy back his health. But like a faulty pipe that torqued over time, his system too would implode one day.

***

Like me, Daddykins used to love gorging on Mrs. Nigam's mean tapioca bites which she served with mint chutney. Our neighbour in Dar-es-Salaam, Mrs. Nigam was a spirited woman with a booming voice that reverberated through the walls of our apartment building. By the time we landed in Dar, a story floated around about Mrs. Nigam and her friend Mrs. Rai who were attacked on the beach at Ocean Road one night. She bit her attacker's wrist so hard that all he wanted was to be let go of in one piece. Mrs. Nigam said later that it wasn't heroism, that she simply did what her body told her to do.

She was a woman of the world who spoke good English and managed to have an easy, open relationship with her four daughters. She was the mother I wanted to be for my daughter decades later, a mother with whom no subject was taboo, not even the penis-toting Mistry in the apartment downstairs.

In Dar, I felt a whole new me emerge. When you live elsewhere for a time, you begin rebuilding yourself, cell by cell. I remember a girl called Julia in fifth grade at Bunge Primary School, a black girl with an afro who was sparky and dynamic. She spoke her mind. She snapped at the boys. When she walked into the classroom, a frisson of fear crested through the room. I wanted to be Julia.

Julia acted out the verses of a rhyme I would read to my children years later in the United States. Like most black women, Julia was already endowed—with rhythm and style—and she used all of her body and soul in the enacting of *Going on a Lion-Hunt*.

> *Goin' on a lion hunt.*
> *Goin to catch a big one.*
> *I'm not afraid.*
> *Look, what's up ahead?*
>
> *Mud!*
> *Can't go over it.*
> *Can't go under it.*
> *Can't go around it.*
> *Gotta go through it.*

And Julia would shuffle, and splash, and slither, and pound, and whisper and thump, as she faced all her obstacles on her lion chase. I remember the lot of us in the class begging her to do it over and over, and each time she would rustle up something new and make us roar. In Dar, as opposed to Chennai, I was among classmates, each of whom was a character, not another cookie-cutter nerd.

While I was being reassembled, my parents were learning to socialise with people who didn't always conform to their values. Many of them loved a good, spiked drink. Most were younger than my parents by at least a decade. When our friends came to our home, which was dry, they made sure they were already sufficiently drunk on beer. The volume would run high. They would be loose-lipped. They tried to ply Daddykins with the merits of drink. Daddykins' blood alcohol content always registered 0.0, but he entertained our friends of many stripes in our home, playing cards, making off-colour jokes, and tolerating their occasional libertine swagger with a cordial spirit. My mother crossed the moat separating her kitchen from the rest of the world. She made friends and laughed uproariously with them in the living room.

Daddykins would narrate many tales of derring-do after those years—of trips to safari parks, Mombasa, Nairobi, Lake Manyara, Mount Kilimanjaro, Zanzibar and Mauritius. I remember many all-day picnics with family friends at Kunduchi beach resort that always ended with watching the Indian Ocean swallow the boiling sun. Towards the end of our stint in Dar, one of the scariest incidents of Daddykins' life took place at sundown a few blocks from our home.

The sun hung low over the waters as he set out on his daily walk down Ocean Road with a friend. That evening, Daddykins didn't realise that he had no money in his pockets. He always remembered to hold on to some change, at least ten shillings, because muggings and petty crimes were rampant about town and an empty wallet was known to have nasty consequences. Realising that it was twilight and that they had straggled into unsafe territory, they turned around and began hurrying towards home, when two men ambushed them. One of them closed his palms around my father's neck and began pressing hard. Under his chin, Daddykins noticed the dull sheen of a knife blade. The other man tugged at Daddykins' empty pockets. Meanwhile, Daddykins' friend begged them to let my father go, waving his wallet at them. Seconds later, they grabbed it and fled.

When my father got home, he couldn't talk. It wasn't clear if it was the pressure on his gullet or the shock of the experience that plugged up his voice box. In a few days, when Daddykins realigned himself, he began recounting a good story of having survived a mugging though it never made as much of a splash as Mrs. Nigam's tale of having chewed up a part of her mugger.

***

Daddykins was surprised how, after a few days of struggling, he suddenly seemed to be able to eat easier at lunch. He told Vinayagam how much he enjoyed his soup. 'I wonder why it's all going down my throat without any problems today?'

'That's life, *Saar*. Some days are good, some bad. We never know what can happen to us at any given time on any given day, *Saar*.'

My father guided another spoonful into his mouth. His man Friday came out of the kitchen holding an orange bowl of curd rice beaten to pulp. He set it in front of Daddykins.

'By the way, *Saar*, in today's *Dina Thandhi*, there's a photo of a man who died last night.' Daddyins glanced up and then continued to work on his food. 'Of a brain aneurysm. He was just forty.' Daddykins expressed shock.

'*Saar*, did you know that all your other spare parts work—even when you brain dies?'

Daddykins looked up, motioning him for some hot water in a cup. Vinayagam handed him the cup.

'*Saar*, they've taken out spare parts for seven different people from this man. They took out his kidney, his liver, his pipeline, his heart, his eyes. Two of those items flew down to Chennai early this morning under police supervision. Apparently, a transplant has to take place within twelve hours after the parts are removed. Did you know that, *Saar?*'

Daddykins shook his head. He set his hot water down and waited for the spoonful to make its way down his gullet while digesting what Vinayagam was telling him.

'And in five hours they took out all the spare parts. That guy may have died but he has made seven people live.' He tapped Daddykins on the shoulder blade. 'Seven people, *Saar!* Imagine that.'

Daddykins nodded, his brows raised in wonder at the singular news briefing from *Dina Thandhi.*

'Any more questions, *Saar?*' Vinayagam asked in English.

Daddykins shook his head. My father who had asked only one question of Vinayagam—why things went down more easily on that specific morning versus all the other days in the recent past—continued to apply himself to polishing off the bowl of curd rice puree.

16

In The Doghouse

Daddykins walked up to me. 'Just look at this,' he said, turning his head to the right so I could examine his face. 'Doesn't this look like skin cancer to you?' he asked, pointing to the dry patch between his nose and his left cheek.

'No.'

'Isn't this how cancer is supposed to look?'

'No.'

'Didn't the Doctor say I might have cancer a year ago?'

'Maybe. But they were suspecting cancer of the pancreas. This is your nose. The locations are far away, like Delhi from Chennai. And the pancreatic tumour was benign.'

'But this patch has been there for months now. What if?'

'Well, you haven't gone away yet, have you?'

~ ~ ~

After Daddykins read about the concept and design of the heritage hotel in *The Hindu*, he was intrigued and so, on a Sunday afternoon in September, Vinayagam drove my father and me into the gargantuan hotel complex inspired by a 1000-year-old temple built by a Chola king. The ITC group had bought a whole quarry in Italy, mined it for marble and shipped sheets of stone to Chennai. I had tried persuading Vinayagam to park the car and join us inside the coffee shop at the Grand Chola but he declined saying he felt awkward. 'Please don't force me, Amma,' he said. 'That five-star stuff is not for me.'

When we stepped inside the lobby, Daddykins sucked in his breath. Awash in marble and fragrant with the scent of fresh roses, orchids and lotuses, the Grand Chola was incongruous in a city where several historic monuments were hidden behind mounds of garbage. We stopped to take in the chandeliers in the stunning lobby, the friezes along the stairwell and balustrade and the gargantuan pillars of which there were reportedly almost 500 across the complex.

While my father's clear vision through one eye made life easy around the house, inside the lobby of Grand Chola I had to hold his hand and help him watch his step. He could not see the glass. I steered him through the place, sounding like a sports commentator: 'Oh no, watch for that glass, Daddykins, you'll lose your nose. And coming up in front of us is the escalator. Right there, yes! Don't stub your toe!' During that hour with my father I realised how much we relied on Vinayagam's alertness when we were in an alien environment.

Before we left Grand Chola, we stepped into the coffee shop by the main dining room. 'I want a cookie,' Daddykins said, pointing to a pink confection in the glass shelf by the counter. I wasn't going to deny him the pleasure.

He bit into a macaroon, a gleam in his eye, the sweet tooth, now in bliss. While I held my breath, he swallowed it very slowly, between hot sips of coffee. If it got stuck in his gullet, it would take over an hour for him to wash it down or bring it out. A few nights before, he had forced himself to go to bed with something stuck in his food pipe. The feeling had persisted until the morning when he awoke; we discovered, later, that the feeling of fullness was also the result of severe acidity and gas in his stomach. But that afternoon, at the coffee shop, bits of the macaroon seemed to slip into his stomach without undue fuss.

'Thank you, baby,' Daddykins said at the end, taking a sip of hot water. He raised his right hand in a small salute to me. 'Thanks for bringing me to this fantastic place.' Then he caught the eye of the girl in the toque who had brought us our coffee. 'Excellent coffee, madam,' he said, smiling, when she came around wondering if she could get us anything else.

* * *

Our black and yellow Ambassador taxi rolled down Parthasarathypuram Road in May 1978 as we returned, now a cosmopolitan family, from Tanzania. Three things would dominate the next two years of Daddykins' life: the state of our house, the decline of his mother's health and the matter of human excrement.

Recently vacated by its renters, our bungalow looked unkempt. It wore the look of a child in an orphanage. It smelt different too, reeking of a film of dust, brittle shoes, aging potatoes and bone-dry dishtowels. The trees around the courtyard were overgrown and straggly. In six years, it seemed that a shroud of indifference had also blanketed the homes on either side of the road.

In the years we had been away, the slums just beyond our home had multiplied as people came into the city looking for work. Right outside our compound wall, with its barbed wire top, the slum dwellers beyond our colony came for their morning ablutions. But Daddykins was determined to drive them away. My father did not attempt to help the slum-dwellers by first talking to them about why they were doing what they did. Instead, he chose an offensive strategy.

He went up to the terrace of our home to find out what time the 'squatters' came to do their thing. When he found out that they arrived as early as 4 AM, he set his alarm and walked up and down his yard to chase the folks who came to plop themselves by the wall. For this, Daddykins set up lights that lit up the entire side yard. The squatters didn't really care if the light shone down on their rear ends. They went ahead. Then Daddykins began walking up and down with a torch right about the time people used the streets. At one point, he lined the sidewalks with glass pieces just to prevent people from walking into the area. But they were a step ahead of him; they began wearing sandals to protect their feet.

One morning a few weeks later, when my father set out to unlock the main gate into the courtyard, he was greeted by a smell that was far closer to him than it should have been. The slum dwellers had decided that if my father was going to give them shit, they would return the favour. Our courtyard was littered with various shades of yellow and brown, a scene that remains etched in my brain as the crappiest day of my late teens.

My father was one of the few in the colony who made an attempt to clean up the neighbourhood while most residents had resigned themselves to the immutability of the situation. I admired his feistiness and perseverance, even though the scatological warfare ended on a violent note. One morning, when my father, dhoti folded halfway up to his knees, was patrolling the streets with a torch light, a stray dog bit him on the shin. For a period of twenty-one days, Daddykins needed a round of painful shots right around his navel for rabies. He lamented that he was in the doghouse at this point and began reckoning that in the land of his birth some things would not go away.

While my parents returned to their old lives, my father's mother fell ill in her home in Palakkad. A few weeks later, my grandmother came to our home to die. I remember the look on Doctor's face as he told my father to disconnect the oxygen supply. My aunt Samyukta motioned for me to bring the brass pot of water in the prayer cabinet. I watched my father pour the water from the sacred Ganga into his mother's mouth. It was the first death in our bungalow.

The verandah resonated with the mantras of death. My father, wet from head to toe, sat with his mother's head on his lap, mouthing them as dictated by his priest. My mother, frozen stiff by the shock of death, seemed to relive the end of her child in her arms. Samyukta wailed, hair cascading down her body: 'No, don't take her away. Don't burn my mother! She cannot stand the fire.' As we consoled one another at the gate of our bungalow, my grandmother's body was carted away by Daddykins, Anandan, Babu and Krishnamurthy to the burning ghat in West Mambalam.

Daddykins seemed to fall ill frequently that year, suffering a second recurrent hernia. I saw him cry often. He wept for his mother sometimes. At other times, he shed tears for Nirmala, especially when he heard her favourite song on the radio. His mother's passing seemed to have shaken many stones loose in his foundation.

* * *

I called Vinayagam on his phone as I walked out of the large glass doors of the Grand Chola holding Daddykins by the arm. My father pulled out his wallet from the right pocket of his pants. He fished out a ten-rupee note. 'For the guard,' he said, gesturing towards the uniformed guard opening and shutting doors as cars drove up and guests alighted or entered the vehicles. 'They expect something, the poor things. Just a little something.' Daddykins hadn't revised his tip since India adopted major economic reforms in 1991. When Vinayagam drove up, the guard opened the door for Daddykins, who slipped the note in his palm and thanked him.

Our car reeked like a sewer. Vinayagam had spent two hours in the parking lot in the basement with the windows down. He apologised for the bad odour and said that the blowers and the air units had vomited out all the junk from the inside of the massive Chola operation and entered the car and soaked into the seats.

We opened all the windows. In a few minutes, we forgot about the smell as I began describing how luxurious the property was inside and how much Daddykins had enjoyed walking through it with me.

I told Vinayagam about the marble quarry, the pillars, and the walls of marble wherever we turned. He listened. But in a soft voice that was rather uncharacteristic of him, he told me his side of the story.

'You see only the beautiful things above ground, Amma,' he said. 'All the ugliness, the wires, the blowers, the machines that hold everything up? Folks like me are forced to see those. Amma, all those fancy pillars you saw up above? I never got to see any of them in the underbelly of the hotel. Because which hotelier will spend on aesthetics down in the pit?'

He told us how most of the time the parking facilities even in upscale malls and theatres were very poor. 'The restrooms for the use of drivers are disgusting even in the fanciest 7-star hotel. There's no seating area. We're forced to stay inside the car. Often it's warm, humid and lonely. Many times, mosquitoes kill us. There's no activity for the lot of us who vegetate in our cars unable to go anywhere, do anything, because hoteliers and others want us to remain underground, unseen, unheard. Sometimes, granted, it's a practical concern. They need us to stay close to our cars just in case our car numbers are called over the speakers.'

He pointed out that deep in its pit, the Grand Chola wasn't that grand after all: leaky faucets, dirty floors, urinals with no privacy and, worse, no water; innumerable wires hanging loose, and sections of the ceiling needing immediate repair.

'And I had no tower for radio. I like to listen to the radio while I'm waiting,' Vinayagam said, looking at me through the rear-view mirror. 'But at least I had cell-phone reception, Amma, now that was a good thing. I could at least talk to my wife.'

In the days that followed, a column I wrote about the seamy side of deluxe hotels like the Grand Chola made the rounds on the Internet. The ITC group contacted me right away and informed me that they would improve the facilities for drivers.

Thereafter, Vinayagam began stewing over his personal safety. 'You know, Amma, you'll go back to America-Kimerica. But what about me? With all the things you write, there may be a hit man out there who has been commissioned to kill me. Who knows?'

On our subsequent visit to the Grand Chola, the marketing head of the ITC group walked out of the premises and apologised, in person, to Vinayagam and asked him about what he thought of the now updated parking garage.

'Much improved, *Saar*,' Vinayagam said in Tamil, blushing, shaking the hand of the suave gentleman in business attire who extended his hand warmly to him.

17

Grab that Rooster!

Daddykins was cold when the temperature fell below 29°C. His sons-in-law seemed to spontaneously combust when the barometer surged over 18°C. Daddykins observed how whenever they visited, their old father-in-law froze to death in his own home in the tropics.

~~~

My husband decided to fly down to spend a few weeks with us. The night before his arrival, my father counted the money Vinayagam would need for the airport trip: 120 rupees for parking and also a tip of 100 rupees that Daddykins always gave him for overtime when he ran airport-related errands. That evening, Daddykins had also left behind a 20-rupee note for flowers for the prayer room for the following morning.

In the days leading up to Mo's arrival in Chennai, Vinayagam had been singing a romantic Tamil song from the movie *Veera Pandiya Kattabomman*. He crooned it as he bustled about between the kitchen and the living room. Sick of hearing the same song for days on end, I asked Vinayagam if he was oddly excited at the thought of meeting the man to whom I had been married for over twenty-nine years. He shook his head.

I had been married long enough for the flames of desire to have been doused somewhat by folding laundry, burping babies, visiting emergency rooms, unloading dishes, fixing plumbing, going under the knife for two caesarian sections, packing school lunches, attending violin and dance recitals, stopping and restarting the newspaper before and after a vacation and opening the mail every evening. Marriage had supplanted the quixotic with the neurotic. A good friend had once remarked that her marriage was built on trust, not lust. I could see why. Housekeeping and childrearing eroded sexual desire as steadily as methane carved a hole in the ozone layer.

I begged Vinayagam to please stop singing on my account for my husband. Vinayagam giggled. 'But, Amma, you're seeing your man after two months!' he said, and then he burst into song again shutting the living room windows one by one so he could turn on the air-conditioner in readiness for Mo's arrival late at night.

When Daddykins awoke at 5 AM, his stark home had been converted into a Google Data Centre. Green lights burned. Red lights blinked. Units beeped. A camera lay, its maw open, its battery charging in a manmade hole in the wall. A black wire lay coiled under the rust-orange sofa. Another crept from the telephone pit to the dining table. A cell-phone rattled.

'There! Your husband's here, I see,' Daddykins said flatly with a cursory look at his upgraded, cockpit-like telephone centre. 'The snakes are out.'

My father worried that the people of the next generation were so tied to technology that they had lost touch with the simplest gestures of human connection, the art of a conversation. However, he also complained that his second son-in-law talked too much as opposed to his first one who talked too little. Still, Daddykins accepted both men the way they were and learned to get along with both by talking to them about the things each of them loved to discuss.

He really listened to them. His first son-in-law was pious and believed that life was dictated by a supreme force; Daddykins had long conversations with him about temples, miracles and the office. The younger son-in-law subscribed to Boolean logic—to 0 or 1, True or False, Black or White—and believed that everything in life was dictated by the availability of broadband; to him Daddykins talked about the next big thing in Silicon Valley, India's strides in high tech and the developments in Mo's company.

The morning of Mo's arrival, when they met in the morning near the bed where Mo lay, they hugged for a long time. My husband was shocked that his father-in-law had shrunk so in less than a year. Daddykins was shocked that his son-in-law had greyed so in less than a year.

Daddykins teared up. 'Thank you so much for coming to see me. And thank you for sparing my daughter so she could be with me,' he said to Mo. 'But, say, can we both leave this room? I can't talk to you standing here in Antartica, can I?'

***

On my first day at Meenakshi College, I told the staff at the office that an error had been made and that what I really wanted to do was to pursue a degree in English literature and not one in Physics as desired and paid for by my father. Daddykins believed, like all the educated elite in India at the time, that there were only four academic fields in the world worthy of consideration: engineering, pure sciences, medicine and chartered accountancy. The rest constituted incidental byproducts, as pit and peel to mangoes after pulp was extracted.

My decision to enroll in a degree in the humanities was one of the two best decisions I ever made. The other decision that I made I owed to my father, although I was far from grateful for it because it presented itself with so much sound and fury.

In the year 1979, I sat under the leafy canopies of the Alliance Francaise with a young man. The two of us met often, before or after college, on College Road in this breezy bungalow with high ceilings, a dramatic porch and a garden area with seating. The young man, an engineer, and I believed we were meant for each other. When my parents happened upon our clandestine meetings, they were livid. Daddykins and my mother were sure that he and I were as unsuited for each other, as a parakeet to a peacock, save for the fact that we were both from the same Tamil Brahmin community.

My father did not believe in love before marriage. All love was infatuation, he theorised, until it was buffeted by the trials and tribulations of marriage. Daddykins accused me of losing my head. 'You decided to go on and get infatuated with the very first male your eyes alighted on,' he said. The minute we landed from Tanzania.' He hollered about all the privileges he had given me. I pointed out that disallowing his daughter from dating someone was not exactly giving her freedom of choice.

My mother, on the other hand, turned barbaric. She told me that at eighteen, I was far too young to know whom I should marry. Reminding her that my sister had likely chosen her partner by the age of fifteen, made my mother angrier still. When stripped of her dignity in any way, she lashed out at her victim with a tongue that could curdle milk. She told me I dared not compare Thalaivar with my paramour. She compared me to all the cousins who were my age and told me to consider bottling and inhaling their gaseous emissions so I could fix my addled brain.

One day, at the height of our detente, I told my father that he was a hypocrite for permitting one romance but snuffing out another. That evening, Daddykins snapped.

'How dare you?' he cried, looking around for something while moving swiftly about the living room. 'I've taught you to be feisty,' he shouted. 'The fellow you seem to be enamoured of will quash your spirit. I know his family.' And, suddenly, in a move that took me as well as my mother by complete surprise, Daddykins picked up a cane chair and raised it high above his head.

His face was contorted with rage. 'You listen to me!' Daddykins roared, moving towards me, while my mother continued to tug at him to calm him down. I accused him of simply wanting control. What he really wanted was to be able to choose a husband for his daughter, at least the second time around, I ranted.

'If you say one more word,' Daddykins yelled, still brandishing the chair, the look in his eyes menacing. Teeth grinding, he lunged in my direction. Red-eyed and teary, my mother ordered me to stop provoking him. Daddykins broke out in a sweat. His body shook.

While I was furious with my father for his rage, for his attempt to control me, what he said did bring to mind something that I had earlier tried to ignore in the man I was dating. The gentleman had disapproved of my excelling at college. 'If you continue to ace your classes, your parents will imagine that you don't care enough about us,' he had said. I couldn't express it adequately at the time but I too felt in my gut that the man I married should be an unconditional champion of my achievements. My relationship ended soon after the showdown with my parents.

I embraced the reality of an arranged marriage even though I was distraught and felt unhinged in the ensuing months. Half way through the year 1983, I had already met nine men, all of them introduced by my father, who tirelessly responded to matrimonial advertisements in *The Hindu*, week after week.

Sometimes, it wasn't clear who the future bride was—myself, or my mother. She had reservations about every potential groom the second he sailed out of the door. One of them was too short. One had a finger missing. Another was old enough to be my father's brother. Another was so morose he didn't seem to own facial muscles. Yet another had a mother who demanded a dowry of 10,000 rupees, for starters, right in our living room, even before I met her son.

A tenth man came along as the year drew to a close. My parents and my grandfather liked the family on sight. Over the course of the year, we had met and talked to many members of his family before we met him in the last week of December. There was a disarming quality about this man that came through within seconds of the meeting—a direct manner and a candour that made him stand out from every other young man who had crossed my path in the past.

Minutes before the gentleman walked into the room to meet me for the very first time, my father slunk into my room to air his views about him. Daddykins had talked at length with him and he had been impressed. He had felt, instinctively, that the lad was just right for me and our family. My mother seemed to feel the same way, he said, adding that if I were bright, I would trap him 'like one would a rooster' and simply never let him out of my sight or my life.

18

Uttarayanam in Palakkad

After each of his many long visits to my home in America, Daddykins returned to India and told tall tales to Vinayagam about a life of "torture." 'As soon as you land, my daughter will chain you to a chair. You cannot move this way or that. She keeps her house so clean that the people who enter her home cannot breathe, every object has an allotted place, and every place has an allotted object. If something that is supposed to be here is moved elsewhere, you've had it. Vinayagam, I'm warning you, don't go to America.'

~~~

In the rising heat of April 1993, Daddykins escorted his father to his home in Palakkad, where my uncle Babu lived. Daddykins had protested before the trip. 'Why this obsession to die in Palakkad, when your old house in the village is not even large enough to hold you and Babu's family?' His father shrugged off his son's comment with a weak smile. He told his son that he would not understand now: his soul was in Palakkad.

Whenever I asked my grandfather about his fascination for his ancestral village, he explained it to me thus: he said he loved to read a newspaper sitting on his *thinnai* watching the world go by.

He was happiest when he visited the sanctum sanctorum of Lord Gopalakrishna at the temple every morning and every evening, returning home with a little tulsi leaf tucked behind his right ear and some sandalwood paste smeared on his forehead. He dreamed, he said, of dying in Lakshminarayanapuram—during those six consecutive months of the year when the sun appeared to travel north of due east, in *uttarayanam*.

Daddykins' father died, instead, in the latter half of the year, unfortunately, when souls were believed to crash headlong into the land of demons. I know that there, my grandfather —who had never passed judgment on anyone other than a politician— would have been a sweet seedless grape among pineapples.

Daddykins' father stopped breathing on a day in early October, before the nine-night festival of Navarathri, right as vendors began rolling carts of painted mud dolls down the village roads. As he took a first sip of tea, his spirit slipped away, possibly through the *tavaram* where his late wife used to stand picking head lice or braiding her daughters' hair, and out through the *thinnai* where he spent many waking hours debating Mrs. Indira Gandhi's dictates, and perhaps up Double Street gliding, in a straight line, into the jasmine-scented home of Lord Gopalakrishna.

Daddykins found out later that on his deathbed, his father had no regrets but one. 'Like all my children, you too deserved a college education,' he had said to Vijaya, apologising for his negligence. In 1945, he had listened, instead, to the sentiment of the village—that educating a woman after she turned sixteen would endanger her prospects for marriage.

My grandfather left behind some small patches of land and the contents of a metal trunk. A few shirts in colours that wouldn't stand out in a doorway on a bright day. Five cotton dhotis. Four undergarments that were just long pieces of cloth—a cotton loin cloth that hung over a cotton string, a watch, a belt, one pair of sandals, his hearing aid (as good as new), a walking stick, a walker, teaching awards, several diaries, his glasses, a plastic box of holy ash, a fountain pen, several prayer books and his own copy of *The Ramayana* and *The Gita*.

* * *

On the morning of a new moon, my father skipped his walk. He showered early to perform a prayer for his ancestors. When Vinayagam rang the doorbell, Daddykins, clad in his dhoti and bare-chested but for his Brahmin thread, was seated on a wooden plank out on the balcony floor. Vinayagam was annoyed that his boss had rushed to begin the observance.

My father told him how he needed to get to the office by 10.45 AM because he had so many important cheques to sign and Vinayagam retorted that he was going overboard and that all this sweating the small stuff was not good for him at all, given his acidity and stomach problems.

Daddykins opened his prayer book to the pertinent page. Vinayagam brought out specific brass vessels and placed a brass pot filled with water by my father's side on the floor.

Before offering sesame seeds to his ancestors, Daddykins prayed to Lord Vishnu and Lord Brahma for the power of the prayer to be absorbed by the black sesame seeds. Then, Daddykins offered the charged sesame seeds to his ancestors by releasing water slowly over the seeds placed in his palm. The seeds fell into the plate.

He stopped, between reciting the mantra, to rifle through the plastic bag that Vinayagam had placed next to him.

'Vinayagam, I don't see any *dharbai* here.' In seconds, he would begin his chant wearing a *dharbai* on his finger. The holy grass absorbed radiation. When used with a mantra, it was powerful.

'*Saar*, look inside,' Vinayagam said, mopping the floor of the prayer alcove. 'I put it there last evening.'

My father rummaged inside the bag again and fished something out claiming it didn't look right. It was a long familiar stalk of holy grass. 'This looks different.'

'It's the right one, *Saar*.'

'No, it doesn't look like the one for Sama Veda.'

'But it is. I told the guy at the shop to give me the one for Sama Veda.'

My father stared at the grass stalk. 'Then I suppose it is the right one, after all.' He fixed it around the ring finger of his right hand and began praying.

'You know, *Saar*, I might as well do all these prayers to your ancestors on your behalf,' Vinayagam said. 'I'll simply let you get the benefit. Why are we pretending? I know most of these mantras now anyway.'

Eyes shut, Daddykins continued to pray.

An hour later, after Daddykins had finished his prayer, he said he felt weak. As per the ritual, he had begun his prayer observance with a fast from the morning. His body caved into his rust-orange sofa when he was done.

Vinayagam handed Daddykins a glass of whipped buttermilk seasoned with asafoetida and salt. My father sipped it eagerly.

'I don't understand why you must do this month after month and tire yourself out,' Vinayagam said. I'd often heard my father wish that he had taken better care of his parents. For Daddykins, the observance was not just a ritualistic duty. Perhaps it was a redress, an act of expiation. But Vinayagam would never understand.

Daddykins looked up at his valet. 'I have to do it in memory of my parents and all those who went before them. To all my ancestors. I've done it for over thirty years now.'

'*Saar*, how old are you?'

'Ninety. Very soon.'

'See? That's what I mean. You're at that age when someone should be doing a prayer observance for you, *Saar*. You're that old. Why should you continue doing this prayer for your ancestors now when ordinary things tire you out, *Saar*? I think you should stop doing these prayer rituals from the following month.'

Vinayagam approached me. 'Amma, please tell your father it's meaningless, at his age. He was the best son he could ever be to his parents.'

19

Life, Liberty and the
Pursuit of Happiness in India

Of late, Daddykins had become irritable. He was quick to rush to judgment. He couldn't differentiate between levity and gravity.

'Daddykins, you've lost your sense of humour,' I said.

'Yes, I have,' he said, a little contrite.

'Any idea what we can do? What's changed?'

'Just take me to America, I say.'

'Why, Daddykins?'

'Anyone can own a gun in America. You can just take me there and put a gun to my head for losing my wit.'

~~~

As his ninetieth birthday drew closer, my father's focus grew more inward. He orbited around himself and his routine. He was no longer enraged by the news when he read *The Hindu*. He had no opinions. Reading had also become an effort.

Sometimes, especially in the mornings, after Daddykins was seated in the living room, shooting the breeze between his shower and lunchtime, Vinayagam conjured up tricks to snap him back to his own old self. A television junkie, Vinayagam soaked up travel shows. Now he had started watching Discovery channel with a voiceover in Tamil. It had opened up a whole new world for him. As he started acquiring knowledge, he began force-feeding it to Daddykins the way geese were fattened for foie-gras. Almost daily, he also shared snippets from *Dina Thandhi* based on which he found something to argue about. At other times he quizzed him.

'*Saar*, do you know which queen reigned the longest? Who is that woman?'

'Queen Victoria. Then, Queen Elizabeth,' Daddykins said. 'Victoria ruled for sixty-three years.'

'Give me your hand, *Saar*.' Daddykins extended his right hand, and Vinayagam shook it vigorously saying how much he was impressed by my father's knowledge. He riddled him with more questions.

'*Saar*, did you know that the first omnibus opened in Paris in 1819?'

'Yes, I believe it was a horse-drawn double-decker bus,' Daddykins said.

'*Saar*, did you know one generation is thirty-three years? But you have seen four generations, *Saar*.'

'Yes, indeed,' my father said, nodding slowly in acknowledgment of something wondrous. We sat in silence for a few minutes. I saw my father as a young man of twenty standing on a hillock, scouting the many mountains he must still climb. And then, almost too soon, it seemed, I saw him standing now at the grand summit, the place I too might reach one day and peer down from not knowing how I ever made the climb. Vinayagam's voice sliced through my reverie.

'*Saar*, the paper says it's raining now in Myanmar,' he said, surfing quickly through the pages before folding up the paper and putting it away on the coffee table.

'Oh. It's raining in Burma. Really?'

'Myanmar is Burma?'

Then, as Vinaygam listened at his feet, Daddykins told him Burma had been part of the British Empire when World War II broke out and how, in 1942, Japan invaded Rangoon, the capital of Burma. The Burmese had hoped to gain support of the Japanese in expelling the British. Then he told him about the plight of Indians in Rangoon who had very few options when the British suffered defeat. 'Some escaped by boat. Some chose to stay back. Many returned all the way to India on foot. So many perished on their way through the forests.' Vinayagam listened until Daddykins was fatigued and could talk no more.

***

It wasn't until Mo and my parents had crossed several miles on the highway out of New York city that they realised that something had happened inside Macy's on Herald Square in Manhattan. When Daddykins asked my mother for her diary, she discovered that she had lost just about all the contents of her handbag.

Four days into their trip to America, they had already been robbed by a retail theft ring operating inside the landmark store. Later, my mother said how while shopping, she had theorised that America was just about as crowded as India and that being at Macy's was not different from being shoved and jostled at Ranganathan Street in Chennai. Daddykins and my mother never tired of narrating that tale.

They regaled the family with many stories of the year 1989, the most adventurous time of their lives, the year in which Urmila and Thalaivar took them, along with their two children, on a luxury bus trip through Europe. Daddykins would ride on a gondola in Venice, stand ashen-faced by Gandhi at Madame Tussaud's, and marvel at the view of the Notre Dame from the boat on the Seine. My father would recount, as he and my mother packed to leave, that it was the year of wishful thinking and magical happenings. They arrived in Boston from London to learn that Mo and I were expecting our first child. Before their granddaughter arrived, something happened, however, that was another first for Daddykins.

In October 1989, I was driving my parents in our Toyota Camry. We had stopped at a red light when the car trembled for a few seconds. The three of us didn't quite comprehend what was happening but we were experiencing our first earthquake. The road rose and buckled like a thick carpet. The lights on Almaden Expressway swayed like a sunflower stalk in a gale. We heard the grate and clang of metal.

I continued driving, instead of making a U-turn and heading back home. The parking lot of the store we entered was empty. Inside, we saw the devastation that 20 seconds had wrought in San Jose, 40 miles north of the epicentre in the mountains of Santa Cruz. All the glass had shattered. The clerks seemed frazzled by the cleanup that awaited them.

When Mo called us from Texas where he was travelling on work, he was concerned for our safety when the home phone went unanswered. In the era when landlines were the only means of communication, Mo was aghast that, instead of driving back home, we had actually sought to drive around to see which shops may be open in the vicinity after we had experienced an earthquake that had registered 7.1 on the Richter scale, especially when, and this was a detail of some consequence, I was six months pregnant.

To this day, my husband's story goes uncontested, but I do remind his listeners that out on the road it isn't ever obvious how acute an earthquake is, especially when one doesn't turn on the car radio, which, according to Mo, furthered proved my extreme foolhardiness and my parents' culpability in encouraging their daughter's thoughtless conduct. Daddykins believed it was a minor matter of a major earthquake blown to an order of magnitude greater than that of the earthquake itself by his son-in-law who, he was discovering, especially as the year of intimacy wore on, was gifted at finding fault with everyone other than himself. Daddykins could never understand his son-in-law's apoplexy as he narrated the tale of three idiots gallivanting on a bad night. Daddykins found his reaction to be of a seismic intensity that Mo would be better off showing 'in the chores that he should be taking up around the house.' After all, we did get home in one piece, Daddykins argued.

That entire week, Daddykins sat in front of the television quaking at the immensity of the damage, thanking our fortune for not having been on a freeway where the upper level collapsed, crushing the cars on the lower deck. He marvelled at the emergency personnel, who demonstrated such a level of care and concern in getting the little details right, following such a catastrophe. In tears, Daddykins and my mother watched the rescue efforts, extolling the compassion of fire fighters and paramedic personnel.

My father was in love with America that month and even after that, especially as he passed the driving test on his first attempt and began driving on California's roads. He admired the law and order and the respect for the pedestrian, and commended the law-abiding citizens who moved to the shoulder of a road whenever an ambulance blared its way through the streets. He told me how exciting it was to drive and feel the tires glide on satin-sheen roads, where people heeded red lights and showed mutual respect at four-way stop signs.

Mostly, Daddykins loved the freedom, a situation in which no one rang the doorbell, where others, like the milkman, maid, the paper boy, the watchman and roadside vendors, didn't slice into the privacy of one's daily life. On his morning walks, he liked to watch the progress of the building of a house around the corner. He was fascinated by how quickly a house rose up from wooden scaffolding—a house made to withstand earthquakes, in barely three months. America chugged along like clockwork, he said, as it should be, within specified timeframes and with minimal bureaucracy.

Yet, at other times, when he couldn't just get on and off public transportation the way he could, say in Madras, or in London, or in Hong Kong, he said life in America was very isolating for active seniors and that the unnatural quiet of the American suburban life was the saddest and loneliest thing for a human being. After a whole year with us, he concluded, like many South Asians, that he found life in the United States daunting. He couldn't fathom why the United States had to complicate the dispensation of care and drugs with the monstrosity called insurance. He began disliking how the field of medicine had been compromised by people's litigious tendencies. There was also the matter of sports, he pointed out. Americans didn't care at all about cricket. They didn't care enough about soccer or tennis. One of his other pet peeves was that in America, he didn't have access to *The Hindu*. The *San Jose Mercury News*, he decided, was a worthless paper for prioritizing the picture of a man hugging a dolphin at Monterey Bay on its main page on the very day that the Cold War ended in Berlin.

Coming to America raised an important question for my father. Where did he want to spend his last years? He believed that until the last day of his life every human being must own a space to call his own where he could live life on his terms. 'In India, I can,' Daddykins said. 'There, I'm the king of my castle.'

20

The Boy who Came to Drive

Daddykins, Vinayagam, my sister and I were watching the colourful 'Beating the Retreat' ceremony, telecast live from New Delhi, on the occasion of the 64th Republic Day of India.

While watching the Indian President do the honours, Vinayagam turned to Daddykins and asked him what he would do if he were President of India for just one day.

'First of all,' Daddykins told him with a watery smile. 'I'd hire you once again.'

~~~

I entered the apartment building in Trustpuram and an old security guard inside directed me to a relative's flat on the second floor. The guard, my relative said, was Vinayagam's father.

When I returned to the car, I accosted Vinayagam and asked him why he didn't think to come up and introduce me to his father. He shook his head, 'No chance, Amma. Please get in.' He reached behind his seat to open my door. 'I don't talk to my father. Nothing left to say to him.' I got in. He sped out of the neighbourhood.

'My father is not going to be around very long,' I said. 'One day yours will be gone too.' Vinayagam slowed down as a drove of girls spilled out of the gates towards the bus stop at Meenakshi College. 'Just forget and forgive,' I said.

'You'll never understand', he said, glaring at me through the rear-view mirror. 'And please don't ever compare your father with mine. That's unfair—to your father.'

We began climbing Kodambakkam Bridge. For a minute, we flew above a city snarled in the messy harmony of ancient temples, roadside flower-sellers, chai stalls and behemoths of glass and steel. Chennai spoke the truth. We could not bury the ancient landmarks of one's past with spanking billboards to our present.

We hurtled down Periyar Road, past rows of mud pots. Petroleum cans molded into tandoori ovens lined the thoroughfare. Vinayagam told me he spent his early years a hundred yards from the potter's colony. His family's one-room tenement, which he shared with his parents and two brothers, stretched into a kitchen, living room and bedroom. Four bathrooms served about a hundred people who lived in the community. The thatched roof over their home protected them during the summer months but during the monsoons the dry coconut leaves didn't shield them from pounding rain.

'My mother would position vessels all around the room to catch the rainwater,' Vinayagam said. 'We'd have to find a dry corner to sleep in because in a downpour the ground would be sodden too.'

'Do you know there are many days in my early years when I didn't have the bus fare to go back home? So I'd leave your parents' apartment, buy some roasted peanuts at Panagal Park for a rupee, stuff the paper cone in my pocket and trudge the nine miles to Porur. I was too proud to ask your father for three rupees.'

At the time, Vinayagam's father could have afforded a better place for his family because he was making good money as a security chief for a hotel. 'Spent it on booze and cigarettes' he said, bitterly.

I said that at least he took care of the basics: food, shelter and clothing. Vinayagam rolled to a stop outside our gate. 'Yes. And that is why I did not kill him, Amma,' he said. 'But beyond the basics, what did we own? Nothing. Not a speck of dust.'

***

Vinayagam was introduced to my mother on a day in June 1998 by Mr. Fancy of Fancy Ladies' Tailor. My mother trusted Mr. Fancy's attention to detail and fit. He tailored classic sari blouses that glided on like a second skin. Even though Vinayagam was employed by a dentist next door, he ran daily errands for Mr. Fancy, buying him lunch and tea and performing other little chores; the tailor had been impressed by the young man's efficiency and he recommended Vinayagam for the job of a chauffeur.

The following morning, his driver's license certificate in hand, eighteen-year-old Vinayagam rang the doorbell of my parents' apartment. When Daddykins asked him if he would be able to drive his Maruti van, Vinayagam told him that he had driven many different cars, although the one that he had been most familiar with was the 86-model Fiat that belonged to the dentist at whose office he was an assistant. What he did not tell Daddykins that day was that he had taught himself to drive while washing ten cars, at 75 rupees a pop, monthly, from 6-9.30 AM at Majestic Apartments in the neighbourhood of Vadapalani. That he had been unable to afford the 500 rupee fee to apply for his driver's license. That a benevolent gentleman whose car Vinayagam used to clean offered to lend him that money. That he had mastered the art of vehicle management while moving cars around in the Majestic parking lot and fiddling with the brake and clutch as he cleaned the cars. That his knowledge was mostly theoretical as when he rode the city buses while seated close to bus drivers to watch how they handled traffic. That he also held down another job driving a milk van, a Tata 207, nightly, from 9 PM to 4 AM.

Handing back his certificate, Daddykins explained his duties: Vinayagam would need to reach the house by 9.30 AM, wash the blue Maruti van, then drive him to the office by 10.30 AM. Vinayagam would bring him home from work by about 4.30 PM after which he was free to leave. Daddykins would pay him by the hour for overtime. His salary would begin at 1600 rupees a month.

Sometimes, Vinayagam would come back home in the morning after dropping Daddykins off and then ferry my mother around on her errands. At other times, he would run errands for her on his bicycle. Vinayagam's expanding duties found him folding into the hollows of my parents' lives. Every week, after a grocery shopping spree, Vinayagam offered to put the vegetables away in the fridge. My mother taught him to wrap winter melon in newspaper sheets before storing it in the fridge drawer. She showed him how to choose cabbage: small, tight, heavy. She supervised him as he cleaned the fridge with soap and water. She taught him how to roast ingredients in the heat of the sun to make sambar powder. She shared her recipe for the spice; he bought the ingredients and carried them upstairs to the terrace in enormous brass trays. Then my mother warned him about crows eating the lentils. She taught him to place weights all around the net covering the raw spices. Later, when he brought them back downstairs after a few hours, she crunched the curry leaves in her fist to show him how they had been baked in the sun.

Two years after he began working for my parents, Vinayagam told Daddykins that he had finally amassed enough money to get his mother a cooking gas cylinder for her kitchen. He also wanted to buy a television. Until then, the only possessions of note in their rental home were three things: an old bicycle for local transportation, an almirah for storage and a mini cassette recorder for entertainment. Daddykins drove with him to Vivek & Company at Bazullah Road to sign him up on their monthly installment programme, paying the first installment towards his television.

* * *

Vinayagam was cagey when I asked him to drive me to his home in Porur, but he acquiesced when I told him that I wanted to get an idea of his daily commute. We set out one morning after dropping Daddykins off at the office. We rolled down G. N. Chetty Road and traced the southeastern edge of Panagal Park until we reached Usman Road where Saravana Stores, Nalli's, RMKV, Thanga Maligai and Kumaran Silks coalesced into a confluence of retail sinfulness. Vinayagam pointed out my cousin a few cars ahead of us in the pandemonium of vehicles. 'There, that's Mala-Amma's car, see?' I was astonished he could even tell from several cars away but when we caught up with them, I spotted my cousin in the back of her vehicle.

'Amma, once I've seen a car, I remember the plate number and something unique about it—a dent or decoration or something that may be special to it. I've never made a mistake. Yet.' I discovered a freakish wisdom in him that made me question the value of a college degree.

He pointed to the bus stop right by Nalli 100 as we shot past the store. 'That was where I caught my 11A bus home every evening—until the office gave me my first motorbike—a TVS Champ, TN09L0017. I still remember the license plate number. See?' He smiled at me in the mirror. '*Aiyo,* for the first time in my life, I flew home. In half an hour.'

At Ashok Nagar, we crossed timber stores. Planks, beams, and bedposts were trussed up on the sidewalk in veneers of dust. This was the Chennai of the bourgeoisie, the cacophonic city of hope for denizens like Vinayagam, who were often mortgaged up to the hilt for a space of their own. We inched behind a swarm of share-autos at the bottleneck leading to Arcot Road. 'At least we're moving today,' he said. 'Some days, it's a parking lot.' We sailed past billboards and effigies of chief minister Jayalalitha and her opponent Stalin.

Every few years, Thalaivar helped him upgrade to a more powerful two-wheeler. 'You know, sometimes Thalaivar can be unforgiving and he gives me a great deal of grief over inconsequential matters. But he is the only one, other than *Saar*, who ever cared to ask questions about my personal comfort.

We exited off Arcot Road, rattling past fields. 'In 2010, I got upgraded again, to a 125cc Honda Shine.' Four years later, he waited several months to get one with the registration 'AP' in the license plate: Honda Unicorn TN10AP2340. 'AP' stood for my parents' initials.

For the last stretch to his home, the road was unpaved. The car clattered. I reached for the hold by the window. Canna plants and banana trees dotted the roadsides. I told Vinayagam that there was no need for us to go inside his home and embarrass his wife. 'Just show me your place from the outside.' Through the rear-view mirror, Vinayagam mocked my bobbing head. 'If you're coming all this way, you must come inside.' We swerved to skirt a pothole. 'They're going to improve the roads but it won't happen that soon. Unless we grease the palms of our politicians.'

His wife Devi was a tall, broad woman with a ready smile. 'A good woman,' he said to me, calling her a scaredy-cat. 'She won't take the city bus from one stop to another. I'm working on her.' While I chatted with her, Vinayagam ran out to buy me a cold Fanta.

Then, he walked me through his small, one-storey house, an 800-square-foot living space laid out with almost no wastage of space, every corner of it functional—a porch, a living room, two bedrooms, two bathrooms, an alcove of a kitchen.

'The day I brought the plan for this land to your father, he asked me to take him home early from work. Then he shut himself up in his room. When he opened the door an hour later, he had redrawn the plan to scale and come up with the alternate layout that you are walking through today.' Daddykins had been appalled to learn of the usurious rates of his moneylender when Vinayagam began building his home. He told Vinayagam to take him right away to the bank; he withdrew several lakhs of his own money to close Vinayagam's loan. Then he loaned him the cash at zero interest and subtracted the money monthly from Vinayagam's salary, waiving a year's payment in the end.

'*Saar* said that to make optimal use of the space, all the rooms had to be on one side. He subtracted space from my proposed living room and squeezed in another bedroom. He considered my future—marriage, kids, joint family, everything,' he said, walking me down a hallway, painted a neon green, that my father would never have endorsed. Vinayagam said now that in so many ways, his dream home also belonged to Daddykins. He took the empty Fanta bottle from my hand. 'His layout worked out perfectly for us, see?'

21

Annapakshi

Daddykins and I were going out on an errand with Vinayagam at the wheel when we noticed that a white van marked SPCA was blocking the driveway of our apartment building. Vinayagam sniffed around the van for a few minutes, and then slid into the driver's seat and released the parking brake. He pushed the vehicle with all his might. It moved a few feet, clearing the way for our car. Daddykins was amused by the scene.

'Little wonder that Vinayagam is named after Lord Ganesha, the Remover of Obstacles,' he said, with a chuckle.

~ ~ ~

The day my mother had a seizure and lost consciousness, Vinayagam carried her across the living room, down the steps into the Maruti Zen, and all the way into Adayar Cancer Hospital. During her three-year fight with peritoneal cancer, Daddykins deflected my attempts to talk about her imminent demise. Discussing it was tantamount to resignation. My sister subscribed to his philosophy, too, while I insisted on using the word 'death' even as they winced.

A year after their vacation in Paris and in Singapore, my mother woke up one morning with a purplish blotch above her eyelids, the first overt sign of an internal malignancy. While he cared for my mother through her terminal illness, Daddykins also watched his youngest brother waste away, between blood transfusions, until, one day, his niece called Daddykins to tell him that it was time to make a decision regarding life support. Daddykins wept. He hoped that when his day came, his little brother would light his funeral pyre. Instead, in September 2002, Daddykins watched him burn.

One smoggy April afternoon, my mother's brain began to swell. She could not tell the time. She forgot names. She did not recognise most people. Her speech slurred.

The Three Roses brought her the sweetest mango slivers. My mother relished them although she looked at her sisters-in-law too with suspicious eyes. She became hostile towards her husband of sixty-two years. 'There he comes, the miser,' she would whisper to Urmila, when Daddykins drove down with Vinayagam from the office to visit her at the hospital. When Daddykins held her close and kissed her forehead, she would glare at him. Disdain turned the corners of her mouth.

One evening, Daddykins asked her why she recoiled when she saw him. 'He loves you so much, can't you tell, Amma?' Urmila said, prodding my mother for a little more compassion towards a thoughtful husband. 'He has been so caring all these years.' Daddykins held my mother's hand in his. 'Yes or no?' Urmila asked in her gentlest tone. My mother nodded, slowly, tears brimming in her eyes. She stared at the clock in the middle of the wall. I saw my mother now, lost in a labyrinth, the door leading out locked shut, the key forever lost.

On a blazing afternoon in June 2005, when my mother returned home after four weeks of brain radiation, she couldn't tell the difference between a blender and a spoon. A week after that, she didn't recognise the urge to relieve herself.

Her maid of many years sobbed over my mother's indifference. 'She used to stand outside the bathroom watching me as I scrubbed.

I got precise instructions every day of the week. I want that person back.'

We too wanted perfection back in our lives. Perhaps wheeling our mother into her durbar would spark that desire to rule, again? My aunt steered her excitedly out of the bedroom, into the court where once my mother presided from dawn until dusk. 'Parvati, don't you want to see the kitchen?' Vijaya asked, pushing the wheelchair. 'Don't want kitchen,' my mother grunted, her voice hoarse, her eyes glassy and distant. She wanted to lie down.

So Vijaya, my mother's oldest friend, led her out of her old den where she once fussed over tiny scratches on her pots and pans, past the Electrolux refrigerator that Daddykins had bought her the August prior, past the dining table with two red HotSpot silicone pot holders from Bed, Bath & Beyond (heat resistant to 675 degrees F), past a two-ply paper towel from Singapore that poked into its holder, past walls of photographs of my mother in the 1960s, when she wore her glossy black hair in a heavy, snake-like braid.

We lowered her gently onto her bed and set her barren scalp on a scrawny pillow covered by a thin cotton towel. Daddykins sat at her bedside, talking to her. My mother stared at the ceiling.

'You used to love collecting beautiful things, Amma,' Urmila said. 'You don't care for any of your things anymore?'

'No,' my mother said, shutting her eyes. 'I don't want anything. Nothing at all.'

During their years of marriage, my mother's material impulses were the butt of many of my father's jokes. My mother's almirahs burst with jars of Yardley powder, Parker pens, elegant copper-bottomed cookware, stone casseroles, pewter cups, silverware, leather bags, glass beads, and saris, each of which would tell a tale of acquisition, return and exchange.

My mother exchanged whatever she had bought at least twice. She strutted into grand retail showrooms with my father, her 'bodyguard,' as Daddykins liked to call himself. She clucked at sari clerks. Soon, the entire inventory was out of the shelves and on the glass counter. She tugged and tsk-tsked at their samples. The sari clerks began talking sideways in hushed tones. Daddykins would dab at the beads of sweat speckling the bridge of his nose. He peeked at his wristwatch. He would run his hands through his hair. Presently, he would begin grumbling.

All the while, my mother surveyed the sari wreckage about her and watched the clerks like a hawk, informing the fellows that of course, a store of that gravitas had more stock in the back that it reserved for its elite clientele and that she being a loyal customer, albeit one of middle-class pedigree, the store definitely owed her and that the clerks had better just go and get the new bundle that they held in reserve. Having said that, she proceeded to install herself on one of the store's wooden benches like a 7th century stone sculpture in the shore temple of Mahabalipuram. The clerks padded back from an inner sanctum in the back of the building, another cumulus of saris in hand.

In her last years, my mother found the perfect ally in Vinayagam. She swore him to secrecy; the sari exchange missions happened after Vinayagam dropped Daddykins off at work. Her eye missed little by way of quality and thus when she said from her bed that she didn't care for anything at all, we knew that she would not be with us much longer.

At sunrise on a Saturday, just as Daddykins finished tightening his shoelaces before his morning walk, Urmila told him not to leave. Daddykins straightened up from the shoe cabinet on which he had been resting. He held on to the door frame of his apartment, leaning against it for a few moments before Urmila led him to the side of our mother's body.

Every day for the next year, Daddykins spoke only about his life with her. 'Did you know that even though your mother was not educated beyond the elementary years, she possessed an innate acuity about people? Did you know she took in everything around her like a sponge?'

Condolence letters drizzled into my father's life that summer—expressing love, sorrow and nostalgia. A condolence letter is one of life's sublime expressions of what one human being means to another. It's a final reflection of a deep dependence, of the ultimate break of a bond, a celebration of what was, and regret at what would now never be.

I remember the glow on Daddykins' face after he received them, his need to share them with Urmila, myself, Vinayagam and his sisters. He gathered them all in one corner of his almirah.

We talked about our mother's candor. The Three Roses chimed in too. When mother did say something, it resembled clotted cream, a blob of unshakeable truth about the world. The Three Roses wondered how she could have flown away, just like that, leaving everything she had collected with so much care. All of us laughed over Daddykins' long-running joke: had it been as easy to exchange a man in those days as it were to exchange a sari, Parvati would have returned him several times for many different men over the course of their marriage.

When my mother had lain in her final resting state, we had swaddled her in a Kanjeevaram silk sari in mango yellow, bordered in red and green threads, with *annapakshi* birds, mystical white-winged creatures that obviated sorrows and multiplied good fortune. Now she reached out to us from her almirah, in tiny whiffs, through the saris that had lingered closest to her skin. We remembered the *annapakshi* yet again, that celestial bird that had nursed all our woes between her heart and her wings and graced us with the bounties of her lush plumage.

My mother's evanescence marked the fading of countless fragrances from my memory, beginning with Chanel 5; the faint scent of Cuticura talcum powder commingled with coconut oil; vanilla potpourri, fresh jasmine, holy ash and sandalwood. I could take a smidgen of all these, boil them together, stir the pot and pour the concoction into a flacon. But how does anyone bring back a mother in a bottle?

***

On a Sunday afternoon, while Daddykins slept, Vinayagam turned on the television and absently began switching channels. STAR Movies was playing *Titanic*. 'Aiyo, not *Titanic*,' I said. 'Not again.'

Whenever *Titanic* played, Vinayagam became distraught as if he was standing out on deck with Leonardo Dicaprio, staring at the murky waters, gearing up for yet another visitation of the enormous tragedy about to befall himself, the ocean liner and all 1500 people in it.

He sat riveted, taking in Kate Winslet's rising and falling breasts as Dicaprio tried to kiss her inside the steaming car. 'But Vinayagam,' I cut in as a cold knife might impale baking bread. 'Just how many times are you going to watch these people kissing and making out and dying anyway?'

He looked up at me, his eyes glazed. 'Amma, I have watched *Titanic* at least fifty times,' he said, one eye still on the car window on which I now saw the sweaty imprint of Winslet's palm. Her hand glided down the window of the gleaming red Renault. 'But every single time, I'm transfixed.' As we watched, he told me that when the movie hit the screen in Chennai in 1998, Daddykins went alone.

'Your father saw it at AVM Rajeswari theatre. Your mother did not go with us because she didn't like to watch English movies. *Saar* got himself a ticket. Only for himself, Amma, and I waited jealously for him outside. The man was gone for many hours. But I made sure to see it with friends a few days later.'

Vinayagam said he fell in love with the movie because it was, first and foremost, a *'nalla kadhai,'* a great story. But he loved it for another reason. 'I like any story about things that move.'

He never got over the last scene. 'Especially at the end, Amma, it's gut-wrenching, when both need to escape but Jack tells her to lie on the door and keep afloat while he just holds on to it, tries to paddle and stay alive in the icy water with just one hand over the door. After some time, she calls out to him. 'Jack', she says, softly. 'Jack!' she shouts again with all her might. When he doesn't respond, she knows deep inside that he is dead, Amma. His hand is frozen, like a shard of ice. Then Rose lets his hand go. He crackles off from the door, you know, like a twig from a dead tree and sinks slowly into the blackness. That scene, Amma, is so gripping, even after a million reruns. It churns my stomach. Every single time. Amma, *Titanic* is an example of true love,' he said, wiping his eyes. 'Real love knows no money or class, you know.' He got up and pressed the switch by the television. Silence diffused into the living room.

Some time after my mother passed away, he and Daddykins watched the movie on television. He said that in the end my father's face was twisted in grief. 'Parvati and I were like this, you know, Vinayagam, he said to me.' Vinayagam's voice was heavy. 'He was in tears, Amma. I don't watch *Titanic* anymore when your father is around because I don't want to upset him.'

22

Once Derailed by
the Butter-Cutter

When Daddykins wrote to Urmila and me, he often enclosed newspaper cuttings of concert reviews, health columns and humour pieces that he had enjoyed in The Hindu. In one of the health advice columns that he sent us, the author—a nutritionist and food writer—had advised readers to do the following test.

"Stand upright and look down. You should be able to see your toes without turning your head or bending forward." The author claimed that many test-takers would not pass it. In the article, Daddykins had made sure to mark up the lines for his daughters, making a note on the side of the column about his own experience with the test: "I could just about manage."

~ ~ ~

In the summer of 2006, exactly a year after we bid farewell to my mother, we got together—Daddykins, Urmila, my children and I—for train travel to Kerala, in the monsoon month of July. We were to attend a cousin's wedding on my father's side of the family, in the coastal city of Kochi. But just as we made our way to our designated platform, we saw our train hissing and snaking its way out of the dock. Daddykins or Vinayagam had made a mistake with respect to train names and timings.

My son, twelve, took aim at his grandfather as we watched the disappearing train, our mouths agape. 'That was our train leaving the station,' he said, narrowing his eyes. 'And you, Thatha, are a butter-cutter.'

'This wedding trip is so not happening' my sixteen-year-old daughter said, with teenage concision, her arms akimbo.

Urmila's lips grew thicker. As the self-appointed matriarch of the family, she often worried about self-preservation in the face of jeering relatives. 'I asked to look at the ticket yesterday. This would not have happened had you only shown it to me,' Urmila said to Daddykins. 'What is everyone at the wedding going to think?' she continued. 'They'll laugh their heads off when they find out that we, the perfectionist family, missed our train.' Thalaivar had decided to jet into Kochi and was luxuriating at a five-star property by the Arabian Sea before driving up to the wedding venue. 'And my husband is going to snicker the loudest,' she said

We discovered that the only available tickets on the next and last train bound for Kerala were in a third class compartment.

'Third class?' I asked. 'We can't get something better?' I sighed. We didn't travel third. Not even second. 'Our mother would never have let this happen,' my sister grumbled, as we finally boarded a grotty wagon in a third class section of the train teeming with families and crying babies. She told me how our mother would have reacted. 'Nothing would escape her eye. Had she been around now, she would have pounced on Dad like a tigress.' She turned to look at me. 'He deserves that sometimes.'

Now there was no one but us left to carp at my father when our plans were derailed. But there was no one but us to console him too. I remembered something my father told me the year we lost my mother. 'There were things that I could tell only my wife and no one else.' He missed her for more practical reasons too—for things as trite as pulling down his vest in the back where he couldn't reach anymore. We were travelling now as the updated family attempting to be whole—with a Brobdingnagian hole blown in the centre of it.

We sat down on cold hard metal seats, pining for the cushioned comfort of a private, air-conditioned cabin outfitted with Aquafina water bottles, fresh pillows and hermetically sealed blankets. Urmila and I had forgotten that we too had travelled in this class on every summer sojourn in Kerala. That was all Daddykins had been able to afford in the 60s and 70s.

At the start of our holidays every April, my mother, Urmila and I would climb into the train bound for Parur. On the return to Chennai, we would have exactly two minutes at the railway station. Besides our luggage that would be spread across three metal trunks, we carted back an aluminum tin of salty plantain chips, a tin of sweetened banana chips, at least two jackfruits from my mother's home, a sack of mangoes from my grandfather's orchard and several brass *koojas* of water inside wired bags. In two minutes, Vaithy, my mother's cousin, would shove us into the railway coach and then, he would run along with the gently moving train, and toss in the tins, the coconut reef broom and the trunks, while we grabbed them from inside the jostling train in which our seats were cold and hard, like the seats the five of us sat on now, forty years later.

We spent the next twelve hours writhing, guarding the compartment's two toilets from which emanated the anesthetising scent of fermenting pee. We glowered at one another. The night grew longer, our sentences shorter.

Daddykins sat sandwiched between two angry daughters. He told us we had grown cosseted. 'You have both been spoilt by marrying men who could afford more than I ever could,' he said, putting his feet up on the seat across from him. 'I am just a retired class I officer from the government of India and I get a paltry sum as pension. You both have hang-ups. And so do both your children.' He shrank morosely into the seat for the remainder of the journey. His two daughters—myself, the Bacchanalian lover of a fine cocktail and my sister, the Grande Dame of luxury travel on Singapore Airlines—sat up through the night, stiff as empresses on a five-layer Simmons mattress atop a split-pea. My sister vowed to not drink water so she would not have to take a leak. My bladder, unfortunately, wasn't made of reinforced steel.

Soon I found myself squatting over a toilet and pondering the fragility of the human condition over a stained, stainless steel hole above the moving ground. I contemplated our bone china egos. Had affluence warped our minds? I thought of something Urmila had said to me many times in the recent years. 'Now that I can afford it, I cannot settle for anything less.' But why couldn't we settle for less? What had we traded it for? When we had not known comfort, our universe had seemed larger somehow, filled with people and conversations. The Alleppey Express was sashaying through country tracks at 60 mph. So was my derriere, which had presently come unhinged from my torso. One of my hands held up the two cotton legs of my pants bunched up at the knees while the other clung to the metallic handle up above, a handle placed strategically so that bodies like mine may not be suctioned out from a speeding train by way of toilet holes.

In the morning, Samyuktha's husband, our uncle Dorai, entered the train at Palakkad, a newspaper tucked in his armpit and a dripping black umbrella in hand. 'Welcome to Kerala, God's own country!' he cried, beaming at the kids. He told them to behold how beautiful Kerala was in the rain. He bade them hurry, and open the shutters, and inhale the green. Through the thinning rain, we saw that the sun had just risen over the paddy fields. Somewhere, between the hot chai he bought us, and our giggles over the misadventures of the previous night and the subsequent delay in arriving at the wedding, was the revelation that it had not been such a terrible ordeal after all.

As we headed back home to Chennai in air-conditioned comfort, I reasoned that journeys were attempts to make memories and that in our moments of jarring discomfort we were always discovering something about ourselves and about those close to us. That grand meeting in 2006 would be the last time Daddykins would see five of his siblings and their spouses; Anandan would have a fatal collapse in 2008. Dorai's heart would shut down overnight just a few weeks later. Babu would begin buckling to cancer in the summer of 2010. By January 2012, Daddykins would be the sole surviving son and, along with his brother-in-law, who was four years his junior, one of only two men in his extended family shipwrecked on the island of dotage.

23

The Creator, The Preserver, The Destroyer

In 1973, I was barely 12 years old and beginning my second year of life in Dar-es-Salaam. One afternoon, right after school, my father dropped me off at the local library. I was returning a book a few days late. I ran into the building and handed the book to the clerk at the counter.

The local Tanzanian rifled through the pages, looking for the tag with due dates. He looked up and told me that I was late and that I would need to pay a fine. I nodded, ready to pay.

'You Indians,' he said, his eyes piercing mine. 'You're all thieves.'

I was frazzled as I got back into the car to tell my father about what had happened. He was livid. But as he drove out of the parking lot, he told me that I should just let the insult glide off my back, that he simply couldn't change the world.

~ ~ ~

Politics. Caste. Privilege. Money. They snuck around like lizards behind the door hinges of our home. Sometimes, behind closed doors, they flicked their tongues and lashed around on the cool marble floor.

One afternoon, after we had fired yet another cook because of her poor work ethic and subpar culinary skills, my father and I argued over why he still insisted on hiring a Brahmin cook. It did not matter, I told Daddykins, whether a non-Brahmin entered our kitchen to cook as long as he or she only cooked vegetarian food inside our premises and met the qualifications critical to the profession: skill, hygiene, honesty, punctuality and loyalty.

Daddykins motioned to me from his rust-orange sofa in the living room. 'I don't relish your pushing me on the subject of Brahmins versus non-Brahmins,' he said in a low voice, his chin taut. 'Especially in front of that fellow.'

I told my father non-Brahmin cooks were more easily available in Chennai. After all, I pointed out, Vinayagam, a non-Brahmin, had been cooking his soup and porridge and his prayer offering every morning. Why couldn't he relax his rules for the hiring of a cook?

'No, you don't understand, baby,' Daddykins said. 'Vinayagam is different. He is cleaner than any Brahmin man or woman I know. He lives by my rules. He follows my etiquette. He runs the kitchen exactly the way your mother did. He has been here for so long that he has evolved with me. He's different.' Daddykins reached out to touch my forearm. 'No. Don't foist your ideas on me. Please.' He paused. 'In any case, baby, I want a Brahmin to cook in my kitchen because that is what my wife, your late mother, would have wanted.' He looked away. 'Also, when my sisters visit, I have to please them too, you know.' His voice tapered off. The justification he had just given me was as tepid as a pot of day-old tea.

I accused my father of hypocrisy. He remained silent. I knew that the Three Roses could be as antediluvian as Daddykins in some of their beliefs. But I also knew that old age had tempered their own expectations, of themselves and of others.

Later that evening, when Daddykins was resting in his room, Vinayagam cautioned me to stop pushing my ideals down my father's throat. 'It's simply what your father is used to, Amma. It's not any prejudice at all.'

Vinayagam told me that everyone in India, not just Daddykins, was conscious of the parameter called caste. People used it to stratify, exemplify, justify and vilify. I had heard how, when socially expedient, Christians and Muslims in India still flaunted their family's caste affiliations from centuries ago when they were Hindus. I was saddened that Vinagayam too had also been brainwashed by the system, by that same mindset that made Indians 'look up' to white people decades after the Raj. I realised what Vinayagam was driving at, that at this late stage in my father's life it was simply not a battle worth having. I was now nursing a deep disappointment in a father whom I held in high regard. He was a compassionate, thoughtful human being, a father I'd always been proud of. But now, months away from death's door, he was unable to shake off his prejudices. The longer I lived with Daddykins, the more I realised that he had changed in other ways as well. His political sensibilities had also altered during the decades I had been away.

On a September morning, when Daddykins was finished with his prayer and seated in front of the television, I broached the topic of his political leanings. He balked, warning me that it would shake the equilibrium of the house. He pointed towards the kitchen where Vinayagam was busy. 'I never bring up politics in that fellow's presence. He and I don't agree on anything.'

'I get it,' I said. 'But you can tell me. Whom did you vote for in the last election?'

'I don't need to tell you,' Daddykins said, scowling. And while I glared back at him in astonishment, he continued. 'Because politics is a private affair.'

Vinayagam came out of the kitchen. 'Amma, your father votes for BJP. Has for a long time now.'

I turned to Daddykins. 'You defected?' I know my voice rose several decibels. 'Daddykins, the Indian Congress was behind our independence. That was the party of Jawaharlal Nehru and Sardar Patel and all the people you and your late father revered in our home for all those years.'

Vinayagam emitted a snort. The television screen closed up on a Carnatic violinist playing a raga. Daddykins increased the volume, while justifying his choice with a growl that always accompanied a discussion of politics.

I remember how late one night in Dar-es-Salaam, when my father's chest was racked with pain, I ran down Ocean Road to fetch Dr. Akhtar, a Pakistani. The Muslim doctor refused to charge us for his house call. My father was moved by the gesture and he praised the hospitality and warmth of people influenced by Persian culture and told me of their largesse as compared to the parochial minds of the Tamil Brahmin community of Madras. But in the last many decades, while watching acts of terrorism on Indian soil, however, he had begun blaming an entire community of Muslims for the viciousness of a handful. Over the Kashmir issue, he chastised the Indian government for soft-pedaling, even as I reminded him that both nations now had nuclear warheads. He never imagined how he might feel if geographies—of north and south, of Kashmir and Tamil Nadu, respectively—were somehow reversed. I was shocked at how a father who used to see nuance had now adopted a brittle stance.

'What has Manmohan Singh done in ten years for our country?' Daddykins asked, pressing the remote again. I snatched it from his hands and lowered the volume. Daddykins continued to sit in grim resignation. 'He's a bobblehead for Sonia Gandhi.'

Vinayagam walked up to me looking sheepish. 'Listen, Amma, all Brahmins in this state vote for BJP. Don't you understand? Because Brahmins here in Tamil Nadu do not like Karunanidhi.'

That was true. Daddykins admired the DMK leader's intellect and oratory but he would bite into a piece of chicken before he pledged a half paisa on Karunanidhi. From the corner of my eyes, I noticed that Vinayagam had lowered himself on the floor behind Daddykins' leather recliner.

'Madman. That Karunanidhi,' Daddykins said, grunting in agreement, now that his affiliations were out in the open. 'He wants college admissions based on caste. Why would I support him?'

I handed the remote back to my father after setting the TV on mute. 'So you do vote for AIADMK?'

'Yes!' he shouted, looking at me squarely in the face.

'You, of all the people in the world, approve of Chief Minister Jayalalitha.'

'Yes.'

'So she doesn't bribe by giving away money and saris in exchange for votes?'

'No,' Daddykins said. He turned his gaze to the television screen on which the violin played a soundless melody. Laughter erupted behind the tall recliner. Vinayagam's head popped up.

'Amma, all parties bribe. Come election time, all these parties shower saris and money in exchange for votes.' He drew himself up by my father's side. 'Your father does not know what's happening in the real world, Amma.'

Daddykins increased the volume on his remote as Vinayagam launched his spiel. '*Saar* is living in this wealthy area where politicians don't need to go out and campaign. Here they have set views. Where folks like me and Saravanan live, things actually happen, Amma.'

Vinayagam made his way back into the kitchen saying he had to get Daddykins' lunch ready. 'Come to where I live, Amma. If you really want to see things, that is.'

I shuffled behind him. 'Like what things?'

'Amma, people come to us supplying, you know, drinks,' he explained, dipping the Bosch's steel hand blender into the cup of cooked rice and lentils. 'They bribe us with drinks. Do you know that come election time, about five days before election, all the TASMAC wine shops are closed here in Tamil Nadu?' He let the blender run for a few seconds. 'Amma, people beat each other up when drunk. To maintain some semblance of normalcy, they close all the liquor shops in town.' He quickly tested the puree with his spoon. 'But what do you think happens then? These politicians simply supply the alcohol under the table, Amma.' He let the blender whir longer a second time. I peeped into the living room. My father sat in stiff silence, the volume turned on high to the NDTV channel. Sometimes noise brought peace.

I could see why, on some topics that reared their ugly heads, Daddykins and his man Friday had agreed to disagree. That was also why Daddykins yo-yoed between expressing affection and anger towards those of us closest to him. Vinayagam's attitude towards many things that Daddykins valued rattled the harmony of his existence.

My father failed to realise, however, especially as illness chewed away his vitality, just how Vinayagam was the daily preserver of his sanity. For over nine months, he had been helping Daddykins in the bathroom right after he cleaned his prayer alcove; every two days, he dropped off clothes to be ironed or he ironed them himself; he dashed down every morning to the store on Ramarao Street to pick up milk or vegetables. When a gas cylinder needed replacing in the kitchen, he called the gas company after he wheeled the old gas cylinder out into the balcony and connected the replacement to our stove. Every two weeks, he carried a 50-pound water can up the stairs and into the apartment. He kept an eye on the depletion of milk, homemade yoghurt, sugar, salt, lentils, coffee and tea and replenished them.

The young man had subsumed every chore of my mother's and, later, of my father's. Still, on some days, Daddykins seemed ungrateful. He maintained that his chauffeur was not indispensable. The monthly chores had begun as duties assigned by my mother for which my father paid a nominal amount as a tip, an issue which, I discovered, was a bone of contention.

It began with what sounded like the staccato of gunfire outside my bedroom one afternoon. The coir rope Vinayagam had used to tie the newspapers with had frayed under the weight. The bundle had cascaded around him as he tried to lift it over his left shoulder. He cursed. He knelt down to begin the process over.

As we drove towards the office to pick up Daddykins, Vinayagam told me about the tip. 'Saar gives me 20 rupees to thank me at the end of this.' For fifteen years the tip had been the same. Vinayagam elaborated. 'I've never asked him for a raise. You can verify this with him.'

Later, inside the car, Vinayagam handed him the 300 rupees he had earned from recycling the papers. As he drove towards home, Daddykins fished out a 20-rupee-note from his wallet and handed it to Vinayagam.

I asked my father why he paid Vinayagam so poorly for the newspaper chore. I told him that Vinayagam had mentioned that the rate hadn't changed in fifteen years.

'Amma, why would you do this?' Vinayagam asked, looking at me in the mirror, aghast that I had elected to bring this up.

'Did you say that?' Daddykins asked, tapping his driver on the shoulder.

'Aiyo, Saar, I never said that.' He stopped himself. 'At least not in that way, Saar.'

I laughed and kissed Daddykins on his temple. 'Of course he said that.'

'Saar, Kalpana-Amma is a tattletale, a troublemaker. Don't believe her.'

Late that evening after Daddykins and I had finished dinner, he called me to his room. He wanted to talk to me about increasing the tip for his manservant, taking into account the increasing chores. He warned me that the increase would be a recurring monthly cost. 'From now on until the end of my life.'

I held his hand in mine. 'Yes, it will recur monthly,' I said, sitting down by him on the bed where the pages of his black diary and his investment papers rustled under the fan. 'But even if you had to pay Vinayagam an extra 1000 rupees for the rest of your life, don't you think you can afford it?' I asked. I held my breath. 'Daddykins, just how much longer do you think you are going to live?' I asked, tweaking his shiny nose. Daddykins chortled. Both he and I began chuckling in the realisation that he was, in fact, hurtling towards ninety in a few days. Another 1000 rupees a month would hardly break the bank.

24

You are Lunch is Ready

Vinayagam announced, as he did every morning with the confidence of Grammar Girl: 'Saar, you are lunch is ready.'

~ ~ ~

Vinayagam approached the prayer alcove a little after 8 in the morning. Old flowers picked off idols. New wick steeped in new oil. New *kolam* etched on black marble. Roses in red basket ready for an offering. Always, a braid of Arabian jasmine. Silver cup with water to sprinkle during prayer. Inside, rose petals floating. In a shiny brass uruli, cooked rice and tuar dhal, ghee-drunk, waiting to be fed to the gods. Chair inside puja alcove. Flame to wick, igniting another day, sooty with uncertainty.

Daddykins, bent now, sculpted in his father's image, sank into the waiting chair. Hands together, like his father before him, Daddykins chanted in Sanskrit. A prayer for peace of mind.

shantaakaram bhujagasayanam padmanabham suresham
vishvadharam gaganasadrusham meghavarnam subhangam
lakshmikantam kamalanayanam yogibhir dhyana gamyam
vande vishnum bhavabhayaharam sarvaloka ekanatham

'I salute the composed Lord Vishnu who is asleep on
a snake bed, the lord of the gods, the support of the
universe, the one who removes the fears of worldly life.'

Daddykins sprinkled holy water from his silver cup onto the
offering inside the uruli. Our gods rarely partook of any of the
rice and lentil. But the animals waited outside by the ante-room
adjacent to the kitchen. Like my mother, Vinayagam fed the
creatures after my father had finished his morning prayer and
offered food to the gods. The squirrels and crows were restless to
eat even as Daddykins braced himself for a meal.

'*Aieiii*, I'm coming!' Vinayagam yelled towards the kitchen.
He tapped the food in the uruli on to the terracotta-painted
wooden slab on the ledge of the ante-room. 'Come and get it.
Caw, caw!'

Days away from his ninetieth birthday, Daddykins, now a
pitted overripe mango whose juice had evaporated, tottered to
his chair. He sat down at the dining table and stirred the contents
of the bowl in front of him. Earlier that morning, Vinayagam had
cut a carrot, six beans and spinach; these he had thrown into the
pressure cooker along with washed moong lentils, rice, salt and
turmeric. Then, he had blended them with a hand blender.

Daddykins lifted a spoon of the bland yellow puree to his lips.
'*Saar*, do you like it?'

'Yes,' he said, pressing his lips together. 'Tasty.' Then he waited
some more, his eyes timid and glassy. 'I feel some graininess,' he
said then, clearing his throat. He looked at Vinayagam. 'Did you
grind it as smoothly as you could?' Daddykins dipped the spoon
and showed him an infinitesimal edge of a lentil that seemed to
have missed the slay of the blade.

'Yes, I did, *Saar*!' Vinayagam's voice grated a little. 'Sometimes
a few pieces may remain.'

Daddykins gestured for water. Vinayagam poured out a glass
of hot water from the flask. My father sipped and waited, his lips

pursed sharply into the air, his cheeks puckered as if he were trying to force down the water to push down the puree.

Vinayagam's face was taut. He moved the glass of hot water away from Daddykins. 'Saar, the doctor has barred you from drinking too much water.'

My father continued to feed himself, half a teaspoon at a time, demanding more hot water with every sip as we watched, frustrated. Vinayagam went back into the kitchen, added more hot water to the puree and brought it back to my father.

Vinayagam was taking my father's inability to eat his preparation as an affront to his culinary skills. I explained to him that even if the lentils didn't get stuck, they were dense, especially for a man with stricture. I told him we'd try another thing that Urmila had proposed. We'd use a heavy-duty mixer to mash up foods. And how about straining everything we gave him? Vinayagam balked at every idea of mine. As Daddykins' health oscillated and as he grew more unstable and cantankerous, Vinayagam became testier. Urmila suspected Vinayagam was buckling under the pressure of multi-tasking.

On some days, Daddykins walked away with over half of his food left uneaten. I saw him once standing by the sink trying to force out a morsel of food that seemed to be stuck deep in his gullet.

As if they were on a daily schedule, two palm squirrels appeared by the window by 9 in the kitchen's ante-room. They stretched their three-striped torsos towards the wooden block. Then they scampered up to the block and began picking at the cooked rice. Minutes later, two crows hovered on the top edge of both open window frames, eyes on the ledge below. In about an hour, the block was polished clean.

***

Now that he was turning 90, he was awaiting a 'big increase' in his pension—40,000 rupees, Daddykins said—and he demanded a weekly trip to the bank.

The morning Vinayagam accompanied Daddykins regarding the pension, no one at the bank had cared that an old man was waiting patiently for someone to address his concerns. They took the papers from his hand but did not cater to him even as he waited in the assumption that they were processing his papers. After a time, when he realised they were not prioritising his needs, he wobbled up to the counter and berated them for being inconsiderate towards an old man.

It turned out that the pension hike was 4,000 rupees— Daddykins had added a zero—a paltry sum indeed as far as the bank was concerned. Daddykins accused the staff of negligence given that he had sent his papers in writing many months before and had visited and telephoned the bank manager several times reminding him to follow up. Then Daddykins warned them that he would write a scathing letter to the Ministry of Finance in New Delhi. Daddykins' histrionics embarrassed Vinayagam who yelled at his boss to compose himself. He tried to drag my father out of the premises. Daddykins then screamed abuse at Vinayagam, irate that his minion would insult him in that fashion inside the bank.

They didn't speak for days following the incident but vented, long-distance, to Urmila until, one day, they began talking to each other again, first, in monosyllables, and then in actions, when, suddenly, it seemed as if the first ray from the summer sun had begun thawing the frozen lake of their communication. It was breathtaking how one kind gesture from one of them spurred the birth of wholesome sentences. Soon each man conveyed to the other how much he needed him for this or for that and the two, the old man and the young man, were bobbing together on a puffy life raft on a placid lake, paddling all the way to an endless horizon.

25

Old Number 20, New Number 90

Daddykins' old city of Chennai remembered the old until the new became
so old that it became the new old.

~ ~ ~

On a damp September morning just a couple of days before we
celebrated Daddykins' birthday at the office, Vinayagam and I
took my father for a spin around all the places he had lived in until
he built his bungalow in 1961. We helped my father into the car.
As always, I sat in the rear to his left.

Vinayagam honked his way into the heart of the shopping
district where Daddykins once used to ride his Lambretta. In
those days, he knew exactly where to turn to reach his destination
but now he seemed lost and timorous. India was now no country
for a ninety-year-old man. T. Nagar had become an unnavigable
spaghetti of one-way lanes, alleys, roads, and flyovers. We cruised
down the road skirting Panagal Park, right by Universal Stores
where Daddykins treated us to biscuits and vanilla ice cream.

Daddykins read road names aloud as we drove. 'G. N. Road!' he said. 'It was called G. N. Chetty Road. And Rangan Street. Used to be Ranga Iyer Street. The blackguards ruling us keep stripping roads of their caste affiliations.' I waited for a castigation of politicians who had deemed it more important to overhaul the road names than the roads themselves. But none came.

Daddykins peered through the window at the spot that was his first home in the city. Doctor and Kunju's colonial bungalow had once marked the statuesque entry to the lane. He had visited the childless couple often until their death, always unable to forget their kindness. Daddykins then spoke of the low wall of the house, the iron gate through which he would enter and the garage across the road. In my mind's eye, I saw Doctor's laugh, his eyelet of a mouth, his rabbit teeth, and the way he sucked in his breath as he bustled around in an office reeking of a compound of Dettol, tincture, chlorine and sterilising metal.

My uncle's home had been replaced by a building with walls that soared like the limestone of the temple at Abu Simbel with a 12-foot tall iron gate flanked by Ionic columns, their capitals embellished by volutes, a tawdry ode to the white and black money spun on the loom of the famous Kumaran Silk Stores.

'Doctor made a neat sum when he sold his house,' my father said. 'But he and his wife never traveled anywhere or did anything. Their cash multiplied and languished in the bank. After their death, relatives tussled over their money. What was the point?'

Unspoken thoughts of my father's legacy hovered over us that morning as we reached an enclave where, seven decades before, my parents had moved into their first rental apartment—ancient West Mambalam, where Brahmin priests eked out a small livelihood. The pluckiest priests graduated to officiating at the celebration of milestones. The unlucky ones, who hadn't sought to pursue advanced Vedic studies, served in the business of death. The smell of gloom pressed over the neighbourhood with its burning ghat.

Priests walked around that morning, Brahmin threads across their bare torso, cloth bag in one hand, umbrella in the other. The hunger in their stomachs welled into their eyes. My father and I watched a young Brahmin cross the road. Vinayagam slowed down. Daddykins looked at me. 'We're all at their mercy,' he said. 'Call one of these poor men and he'll arrive at our home in his thin dhoti with all the things he'll need for cremation.'

Vinayagam waved his hand. 'Amma, every Brahmin priest, rich or poor, attends to all ceremonies, both life and death.'

He had a point. Judging by how Daddykins shifted in his seat, I knew that he too had heard.

'If priests performed death rituals alone, they'd die in hunger while simply waiting for people to die, Amma.'

'My priest does not perform death rites,' Daddykins said matter-of-factly. The top rung of Brahmin priests claimed that they preferred to dissociate themselves from death. Clients like Daddykins preferred not to know.

'Of course your priest does,' Vinayagam said, swinging left. 'He won't tell you that, will he?' He turned to catch my eye for a second. 'Money talks, *Saar*. But death is part of life, after all. We all have to go one day.'

I sat between them, one ear to Vinayagam's declarations and the other to Daddykins' proclamations. In this ancient town, once a forest of sacred bael and bilva trees, Brahminhood had dug its roots so deep and wide that no man, Brahmin or otherwise, could untether the notion of caste, propriety and entitlement from the land that bred them.

Passing several one-room tenements advertising space for rent, we arrived at Subba Road—a road my father remembered as Subba Reddy Road—where it intersected with the alley he had lived in with his young wife. We looked for the first home at Kasi Viswanathar Koil Road. Daddykins could not recognise it anymore. It had traded hands. But he remembered the lay of the land.

Vinayagam helped Daddykins out of the car. For the rest of the way into the 400-year-old Shiva temple, I led him by the arm through the alley abutting the temple, a lane six-feet-wide where a car would not go. Bicycles and scooters skittered past. Motorcycles brushed against my sari palloo.

At the altar, Daddykins prayed. It had been many decades since he had stepped in. The temple gong sounded, sonorous with memories of people past. Daddykins said he could never forget the daily peals of that bell. Didn't they say that sound was the last to go?

I asked my father if he remembered walking down the lane by the temple. Daddykins laughed. 'What kind of question is that?' he asked without exactly addressing my question. He did that a lot. There were many other questions I wished to ask but didn't dare to. I wondered whether my father remembered his bride of sixteen, waiting for him to return home from work. Did thoughts of sex ever trouble the old man? Did the death of his spouse when he was eighty-three, extinguish the last cinders of amorousness? When did people actually die? When we stopped feeling the need to love? Or lust? Or procreate?

As we drove through old roads, typical Chennai addresses jumped out at us. The Madras of then mating with the Chennai of now. A zygote afloat from the fusing of the old and the new: Old Number 25/New Number 47, Hanuman Koil Street; Old Number 64/New Number 47, Ganapathy Street.

We reached Parangasapuram Street where Daddykins had once rented a portion from his cousin Sundari. An old neem tree arched over the road. My aunt Sundari, Doctor's sister, was the fair, Cuticura lady, who walked in a cloud of talcum powder intimidating all who crossed her path. 'I was so fond of Sundari and she of me. But she had her faults. I would just listen through one ear and let out through the other,' Daddykins said. 'That is the best policy in life.'

I wondered how I would feel when I was my father's age, when every link of mine to my past was severed because all the stars I had orbited had lost their light, one by one. Did he feel alone, unmoored, as if he were afloat on a raft in the middle of the ocean with no land in sight?

I heard Daddykins chuckle by my side. He observed that he would not have known where he was had he been dropped blindfolded in Sundari's neighbourhood. Today, in place of her expansive home, a Snack Shack sold pizzas, shakes and burgers.

We flew down the shopping souks of Pondy Bazaar, shooting past a row of garland makers and crossing Mount Road into the alleyways of Mylapore. Near Bazaar Road, Daddykins and my mother had eked out a life together for eight months by stores selling Ayurvedic remedies. Shops here still reeked of musk and incense. I inhaled. My breath filled with vetiver, coconut oil, ashwagandha, pippali, cardamom, nutmeg, and saffron.

We returned home through the side roads of Jeeva Park. Auto-rickshaws had lined up like languorous coaches at the railroad yard. The drivers were asleep, some spread lengthwise on their seat, head hanging upside down, arms slack, dead to the world, like demon Hiranyakashipu on Lord Vishnu's lap.

Vinayagam rolled to a stop. As we led my father home up the eighteen steps into his apartment, I thought about everything that he still wanted to do even though he was turning ninety the following week.

He wanted to fly to Singapore to play with his four-year-old, great grandson as soon as his health stabilised. He wanted to see my overhauled backyard in California. He wished to live long enough to see my daughter married; if not that, he wanted to be present at her engagement, at the very least. Then he wanted a red T-shirt to wear to Jeeva Park, a striking one in carmine, he said, that would turn heads.

On the afternoon of his ninetieth birthday, Thalaivar and his staff ordered a cake that said 'To Infinity and Beyond.' Employees walked up to Daddykins and shook his hands. They hugged him. They teared up. Some fell at his feet. Daddykins was gracious throughout, although he seemed preoccupied. I sensed my father's foreboding. I knew that inside his ninety-year-old shell he still heard the echoes of a youth at twenty; he wasn't raring to prove his mortality anytime soon. While driving back in the car after the party, he turned to my sister to ask her the one question that seemed to be giving him heartburn. 'Was this a birthday or a sendoff?'

26

Die Another Day

Twelve weeks before Daddykins died, when the heat was rising to a broil, my sister told visiting cousins that she was considering hiring the services of a palliative care team to oversee our father's care.

Daddykins cut her short with the knife-edge of his tongue. 'Palliative care?'

'Yes,' she said.

'But I don't need that.' Everyone fell silent. No one dared look at Daddykins.

'Who says I need palliative care?' Daddykins said. 'That's for people who are going to die.'

~~~

Following his birthday, my father resembled a mammal in estivation. Like a wombat in dormancy, he was in a state of suspension from the real world, rationing the use of stored energy. Except for the two hours when he seemed to will himself to go to work, he was simply going through the motions of existing. Daddykins' diet had now been watered down to coffee, tea, clear soups and Ensure.

He still read the *The Hindu* in the morning after a 20-minute walk. The bank complained that his signatures didn't look like his hand. He was irregular with jotting expenses in his accounts book. When the Three Roses and a few other friends and relatives called on the phone to talk, Vinayagam stopped handing the telephone to him. When they asked to hear Daddykins' voice, my father talked to them in a disembodied fashion, speaking in euphemisms about his health.

I sensed his estrangement from the world in other things too. He didn't listen to music; he stopped telling us what was going on at the office. He spent long hours in his room shuffling papers or looking for things. Daddykins seemed lost in his own home.

One evening, I found him in that state in front of his open almirah in his bedroom. He couldn't find the salary envelope for Vinayagam. He hobbled over to the bed and sank into it. 'Please pardon me,' he said, looking helpless.

I sat down next to him and stroked his head, feeling a few errant white hairs beneath my fingers. I hugged him. In my arms, he felt like a seashell on Marina beach. I heard his heartbeat in the hollow of his chest.

The night before, Daddykins had counted Vinayagam's salary several times. He had given me the recycled window envelope with the money. I had verified the amount, marked it 'Vinayagam,' shown him the envelope and then put it away, in Daddykins' presence, in the left side of his drawer.

I got up and walked over to his almirah and pulled out the envelope. His face flushed with relief. 'You know, sometimes I do want to die,' he said taking the envelope, frustrated about his increasing dimness. He looked up at me. 'But then I realise I cannot leave this world.'

'What's holding you back?' I asked.

'I have two girls. They are still young,' he said. 'They need me. I cannot die.'

In most countries, my sister and I would now qualify for retirement. On application forms, Urmila, who had three grandchildren with a fourth on the way, had almost reached the ceiling on age checkboxes. I was fighting to stay at the checkbox marked 'Age 55 and below.' But Daddykins believed we could not take care of ourselves. I kissed him on his forehead.

I wondered why humans couldn't be like the African wildebeest that moved on, sometimes leaving its injured child to be eaten by the lion. The faces of my two children swam up towards me for a second. Articulate. Stubborn. Mature enough to trounce my opinions. Old enough to live on their own. Possibly bold enough to buy condoms and get drunk. But my daughter and my son would be my babies until the day I died. That night, I understood exactly what my father meant.

Daddykins suffered several setbacks the week of his birthday but we managed to ferry him on a day trip to the shore temples of Mahabalipuram, forty miles away. Vinayagam drove us. A flask of hot milk, a diaper, some Ensure powder in a Ziploc bag, a few towels and a box of tissues and water, and we were ready to drive off one weekday morning after commute traffic thinned on the roads.

Miles of brown casuarinas separated the spanking highway from the Bay of Bengal. Urmila told me how in the tsunami of 2004, those casuarinas had buffered the coast from extreme damage.

The grizzly tree reminded me of Daddykins. He had planned ahead for most emergencies. His small investments had paid regular dividends so he could live his life in his way without having to depend on his girls. The day after our mother passed away, my father transferred his apartment to us. He had returned home after the paperwork, his crooked smile belying his sadness at having entered a new phase in his life as a widower. 'As of now, I'm truly homeless,' he had declared, even as my sister and I reprimanded him, crushing him between the two of us.

I imagined myself returning to an apartment still charged with the exoskeletons of his life—his T-shirts, his favourite pair of walking shoes, his belt, his handkerchief, his glasses, his pen, his watch. I would witness his smile once again through his dentures, those beaming bridges to a lost youth that would never let the shape of his laughter dissolve. I felt alone. When my mother passed on, she gouged out parts of me to take with her. Daddykins' death would carve out yet another chunk of my being.

We began seeing signs for Mahabalipuram. All around us, palmyra and coconut trees poked into the sky, silhouetted against wisps of white clouds on the powder blue yonder, just as they lined every highway from Kanyakumari through to the Deccan Plateau. From birth to death, these were omnipresent in our home in many forms. Woven palmyra baskets had lined my mother's pantry for years. She'd used them for storing tamarind and rice; she dried spices in the sun in palmyra sifters. As long as she had lived, coconut flesh presented itself on our dining table daily as both garnish and gravy. The scent of coconut oil lingered on her skin. It was Daddykins' aftershave.

The palms fell away behind us. Stone statues took my breath away, preparing me for what awaited us by the waters. On either side of the road, Ganeshas danced. Elephants guarded the pack of gods and dancing maidens. Seated Buddhas waited under jacaranda trees, in eternal recline, battling the exhaust from diesel and the heat from the tropical sun.

'Amma, you know that stone Ganesha in our puja alcove to which your father offers a chrysanthemum every morning?' Vinayagam said. 'Your mother bought it here, on this road, after haggling with the sculptor.'

Crows cawed. Water crashed against the sand. The scent of salt clung to the edge of a light breeze. Daddykins retired to the stone bench a few feet away from a young couple in love.

Mahabalipuram had been a bustling seaport during the time of Ptolemy. We walked towards the ruins. In the distance, the temple pagodas rose, stenciled in muddy-brown. The rocks had transcended the bids of kings and the moods of the sun, their youth forever locked in the elephantine memory of ocean and sky.

I turned back to look at Daddykins on the bench. His shawl fluttered in the wind.

27

Email Me at Yamalokpatam.com

Daddykins maintained that when he passed away, he would land up in another city, Yamalok, the Hindu equivalent of Hell, whose ruler was the Hindu god of death, Yama. He followed the naming conventions of the British Raj in his regular references to this city of the afterlife (as in Seringapatam and Masulipatam).

Everyone in his circle of family and friends knew that should we ever wish to contact my father in the afterlife, Daddykins' email would be his formal name, with both his initials, of course, @Yamalokpatam.com.

~ ~ ~

Daddykins went back to the hospital for another endoscopy to dilate his esophagus. A few hours after the procedure, he complained of feeling cold. He told Urmila that he felt an odd sensation in his left arm. The water he was drinking dribbled down the left side of his mouth. He could not swallow. He became too weak to move.

Once again, my father had suffered a stroke. This time, he lost the use of his left arm and leg. His mouth drooped even lower.

A seesaw gone awry. A once-smiley, its whistle broken, its lip teetering to the floor of its face.

In the few seconds that the light in his brain flickered, my father spiralled into a vortex of darkness. The doctors didn't believe he'd survive the stroke at his age, given his medical complications.

In November 2013, for yet another time I flew across the Pacific not knowing what would await me at the other end. In the nine weeks I'd been away, my father had lost more weight. He was ashen. His left arm was in a cast. A catheter and an IV unit anchored him to the mortal world of unnatural living. His chest was congested. When he moved half an inch, an oxygen monitor beeped. Apollo Hospital was to Med-India what the Airbus wide-body, double-deck jetliner was to the Wright Brothers' Flying Machine. Daddykins was cocooned in the Platinum wing.

I couldn't quite understand my father's speech anymore but he certainly had a lot to say as I sat in the leather chair by his bed. 'I was telling your sister that I've had a great life, that it's time to go and that you both should let me go.'

'She told me,' I said, caressing his palm. He kissed my hand. My sister and Thalaivar had warned me that he would only talk about Palakkad.

'And I would like to donate money to my village in Palakkad for a new chariot for the temple to Lord Gopalakrishna. It'll be a gift from our family. Thalaivar said he would arrange for it.' Daddykins told me he also wished to talk about his cremation rites.'

'Urmila and I discussed it last year,' I said, touching his chin. 'When you were sick last October at Med-India.'

'You did? Then?' Daddykins seemed taken aback that his daughters had already talked about bundling him off to Yamalokpatam. Dribble always drained at the edge of his lip now. I wiped his mouth with a tissue.

'I told her Thalaivar should perform the rites,' I said to him.

'Do you think my sisters would mind?' he asked, coughing, waving his hand vehemently to signal that there was gunk in his lungs. Vinayagam, who was reading *Dina Thandhi* by the window, dashed over to the bed with a box of Kleenex. As I held the kidney tray below my father's chin, Vinayagam wiped the inside of his mouth and discarded his tissue in the tray.

'I think it should be what you want, given that you have the choice in making these decisions. How many of us get the chance?' I asked.

He laughed, appreciating my candour, I guessed, in matters concerning his mortality. He lay back. Then, in a sudden move, Daddykins slid his torso to the edge of his bed. 'Can you just get me out of here?' he shouted. His right leg was on the floor. 'I have to get back home. I need to go to the office.' Monitors beeped. Vinayagam shouted. I yelled. We pinned him down to the bed. A nurse rushed in. Daddykins sank into his pillow in sullen resignation.

Three days after the stroke, *Physio-Saar*, a physiotherapist, arrived at my father's bedside. My father told him he needed to go to his village in Palakkad as soon as possible and *Physio-Saar* reassured him that, yes, of course, he would have him walking in no time. He lifted Daddykins' left arm and counted for a few seconds before he brought it back to resting state.

Every morning and every evening, Daddykins walked the length of the Platinum wing with *Physio-Saar*. Daddykins was now identified by a number on his wrist—a wisp of a ninety-year-old male in white stockings and blue polka-dot gown open down the length of his back. While *Physio-Saar* held him on his left and Vinayagam on his right, Daddykins began learning how to walk again.

When Daddykins was stronger, Urmila and I would run over to the other end of the corridor. From thirty feet away, we would cry out to him to look up, look ahead and try. And he would lift his chin and look into the distance and smile his crookedest smile, seemingly wonderstruck when he reached where his girls stood. Slowly, he and his walking companions traced their way—left, lift, place, right, lift, place, look up straight—back to his room and his bed.

My father would need a full-time nurse to care for him at home, someone who would be extraordinarily patient with him. Someone who would sleep in his room, change him and keep him comfortable and dry, someone who would listen, who would absorb like charcoal, who would take everything in and let nothing out. For the first time in his life, my father would not be able to climb the stairs into his apartment, or walk to Jeeva Park, or walk to and from the bathroom.

We found her—a girl, Bindu, three months younger than his youngest grandchild. She held his hand.

'Thatha, I can look after you, no problem,' she said, calling him 'grandpa'. She said my father reminded her so much of her grandfather back in the village. Bindu was dark. She was darker than Vinayagam. She was darker than Saravanan. She had long eyelashes and a dimple on her left cheek. At nineteen, there was composure on her pretty face. Bindu's life had hardly begun but it had already been marred by endings. In her last job, she had nursed a cancer patient through the last six months of his life.

On sleepless nights, Bindu sat up with Daddykins. He would tell her stories about his life. One night I overheard him admitting his faults. 'But I want to tell you that I'm not a bad man. I don't lie,' he said from his spot on the bed while Bindu sat on the floor with her chin resting on his bed. 'I don't cheat. I don't molest women. But I admit I have a caustic tongue. I suppose I can hurt people because I'm short-tempered. But that's about it.' Bindu laughed and touched his cheek. 'That's perfectly okay, Thatha,' she said.

One morning, after taking his last sip of coffee Daddykins motioned to Saravanan. 'Could you please bring me my coffee? I am waiting,' he said. He had forgotten. I had just heard the inaudible snap of a cord mooring him to our world.

The great symbol of hope was *Physio-Saar*. When *Physio-Saar* arrived for therapy, Daddykins' mood altered. If, on some evenings, the therapist called to say that he was held up at the hospital and would not be able to visit, my father became dour. 'Irresponsible man. He has no idea how he's affecting an old man's recovery,' he grumbled. 'Does he know he's impeding a man's progress? I need to get back to the office. And I have such important business in my village in Palakkad.'

Daddykins concentrated hard during his hour of therapy. My father's greatest challenge, *Physio-Saar* explained, was to tell the brain to teach the left hand to lift it high above the head. Daddykins would lift his right hand instead. My father was learning to build a link between his left arm and brain; he was using the code between his right arm and brain to apply it to his left. Daddykins' neurologist was astonished by his patient's focus. 'I'm yet to see another man— even one who is in his seventies or his eighties—with your father's optimism and fighting spirit. No one in the medical community will believe he's doing this at ninety.'

A few weeks later, *Physio-Saar* brought equipment that began reactivating my father's nerves. Little by little, Daddykins began to feel life in his fingers although he never recovered sensation in his index finger. After a few weeks of physiotherapy, he was able to lift his left arm high above the shoulder. But his forearm flopped. He was permanently damaged by the stroke in countless other ways. When presented with the newspaper in the morning, he'd stare at it for a few minutes, reading the same lines again and again before losing interest. He didn't ask about Jeeva Park.

He stopped enquiring about his family or the world outside. He was lost in his past, in himself, and Palakkad was the only thing he felt any zeal for. Sports drew out his old self for a time. We prayed for one-day cricket and tennis on TV. Late in January, on one evening during the Australian Open, Daddykins became his sprightly old self, watching Roger Federer play against Andy Murray. A Federer fan, Daddykins claimed that he didn't like Murray because he was Scottish and they were 'all so arrogant.'

That evening, as always, Vinayagam played the role of the sports commentator.

'*Aiyo*, Federer, don't hit a fault!' he yelled at our Sony Bravia. He turned to me. 'The problem is our man always hits the net.' Vinayagam knelt by Daddykins' black recliner. 'Look, it's 30-15, *Saar*, are you following the game?' Daddykins nodded and continued staring at the television screen. Bindu sat in her usual spot on the *diwan* on my father's right. I lounged on a rattan chair a few feet away from Mo who sat at his usual spot on the rust-orange sofa, his computer open on his lap.

At one point during the match, Daddykins told us not to breathe. Federer's going to hit the ball, he said. Federer slammed the ball. The house came down in Rod Laver Arena.

Vinayagam shot up and screamed. '3-2 for Federer!' He clapped. And Bindu clapped. And I clapped. And Mo clapped. Then Federer thwacked another point. 'Yes! 4-2 now! Yes!' Daddykins could not clap. But he lifted his right hand high into the air over the top of his recliner. 'Yes! 4-2. Federer, enough! Stop!'

Vinayagam turned to talk to me. 'Amma, your father and I watched every game—Australian Open, French Open, US Open and Wimbledon—together. He taught me the rules. We used to set our alarm clock to get up in the middle of the night to watch our favorite games. FIFA World Cup. Grand Slam. World Cup Cricket. We used to be crazy like that.' For years Daddykins bought himself the best seat at the Nungambakkam Tennis stadium to attend a whole week of Chennai Open.

Then, as we went into commercial break towards the end of the game, Vinayagam called out to Mo who was tapping away into his keyboard. '*Saar*, my boss has taught me everything there is to know about tennis. But now he doesn't even know the rules anymore. *Saar*, do you know that this is much like a banana plant giving birth to its sapling?'

Fully in the spirit of things that day, Daddykins cheered for Federer while insulting Murray. Perhaps it worked because at the end of a tense match, his beloved Federer emerged the victor. Now Daddykins was delighted to have a semi-final between Federer and Nadal to look forward to. But he was angry because Federer didn't show the grit of his old game.

'Go home now,' he grunted to Federer as his square face loomed into view on television. 'Your wife's going to have your head, I'm telling you.' Then he turned to Bindu. 'I'm so fatigued now after watching this fellow win.'

'*Thatha,* but you didn't play,' Bindu said, hugging his frail shoulders. 'They played.'

'Yes, I know. But it's so easy to tire out when you're watching tennis. Especially a game like this where it took that *mutta payal* took two hours to win one silly point.' Daddykins patted her head. She laughed. Her white teeth sparkled against her pretty black face.

'Anyway, all this has made me hungry,' Daddykins said, looking at Vinayagam and Bindu. 'And I need to celebrate this victory with some Ensure.' His face now wore a woebegone look. 'Please?'

One morning, Daddykins walked again. *Physio-Saar* and Bindu stayed close on either side of him but they did not hold my father as he walked towards the dining area from the living room. 'There, let me walk towards her,' he said to me, pointing to a laminated photograph of my mother on the living room cabinet. 'She was my inspiration to resume walking.'

Daddykins lifted his left leg consciously and walked with his arms up and down, as if he were a soldier in an army regiment enacting a drill. 'Walk normally, *Saar,*' *Physio-Saar* reminded him. Daddykins continued to walk as if he were part of a military unit.

'Great! Now let's walk towards mother's other photo, Daddykins,' I said as my father walked past me. 'Look, she's on that wall too,' I said, pointing to the collage of our family out on the dining room wall.

'Yes, there she is, my inspiration,' Daddykins said to *Physio-Saar*, stopping at the wall to point to a photograph, in black and white, of my mother in a pensive mood. He stood there with Bindu and *Physio-Saar*, staring at another photograph of himself and his wife taken a few months after their wedding. Daddykins, twenty, in a formal western suit. My mother, fourteen, in a sari. Both looked timid, a little anxious, perhaps, as news about the end of the World War and the allied troops readying for D-day came in through the wires.

My father's face creased into a smile. 'Yes, your mother was an inspiration, but many times she was a source of my perspiration,' he said, as he stood by the collage crumbling in toothless glee, his late wife frowning behind him. *Physio-Saar* laughed aloud. Then Daddykins turned around, doddering, his crooked lips careening on his chin.

On days like that, my father seemed rooted somehow. He seemed to listen to the heartbeat of the city and the nation. On another similar day, while seated next to me, my father realised, all of a sudden, that it was almost the last day of the month of January.

'You mean it is January 30th today?' he asked. He burst into tears. Bindu rushed to his side by the rust-orange sofa. I stroked his head. Daddykins said he felt just as he had on that same day many decades ago. That same feeling of intense sadness. Of a helplessness about people and the cruelty of one man towards another.

'I didn't feel so bad when Jawaharlal Nehru went. But Gandhi's passing...' he said, poking a bony hollow in front of his heart. 'It still hurts me here.' And Daddykins sat there, his face puckered in like a drawstring purse pulled all the way. And Bindu hugged him and pulled his pale left hand to her chin. '*Thatha*, you mustn't cry.' She called out to me. 'Auntie, look, he's still weeping.' Daddykins motioned for Kleenex. Bindu fished one out from the box on the coffee table. She wiped his nose.

'I'm going to miss this girl so much when she leaves,' Daddykins said to me. He turned to Bindu. 'When you get married, I will attend. I promise.' Whenever Bindu described her village near Mayavaram to Daddykins and to me, her eyes sparkled and through those two points of light, I saw rice stalks swaying in the breeze and cows ambling, their painted horns fading in the blitz of sun and rain. I doubted that Daddykins would live to see her wedded. Bindu blinked away her tears. She kissed his limp hand.

Vinayagam, who sat by the television, snickered and wondered aloud, in his crass way, about who was going to accompany my father to the hinterlands of Bindu's village. 'Not me, Amma,' he said. 'I guarantee you.' As far as Vinayagam was concerned, the only trip he would accompany my father on was a trip to Palakkad in February. 'After which I think your daddy will have to think of packing up in the direction of Yamalokpatam.' He pointed to the heavens and gave me a wicked grin.

28

The Remainder

Daddykins was pacing the width of the house with Physio-Saar on his tail. He braked, suddenly, just as his valet dashed out from the kitchen into the dining hall en route to the fridge.

Vinayagam shouted out a warning. 'Saar, steady! Why is your truck keeling over?'

'Another big truck came in my way, that's why!' Daddykins shot back, torching his underling with his incinerator eyes.

Vinayagam laughed out loud. 'As I always say...maadu yelachaalum kombu yelakkadhu, Amma!'

Vinayagam's Tamil proverb on bovine resilience defined my father's spirit: 'The cow may waste away. But its horns never die.'

~~~

Daddykins told Thalaivar that when he began walking without assistance he would travel 300 miles west to Palakkad to stay five days with Samyuktha. There he would greet his deity, Lord Gopalakrishna, at his village temple; with Thalaivar's help—and here he looked pointedly at Thalaivar who returned his gaze—he would defray one day's cost during the week of *Ther*, the annual chariot procession down the streets of his village.

Thalaivar held Daddykins' hand and smiled. He told him he would hire a helicopter to fly him in if needed. I wondered if Thalaivar knew that a Eurocopter EC135 went at the rate of $4000 per hour. Daddykins' forte once was to audit and control Thalaivar's expenses; now he wouldn't give a fig if Thalaivar had to rent a jumbo jet to fly him to Palakkad. My brother-in-law was now dealing with an accountant who had lost the ability to count.

One morning, Daddykins gave Vinayagam 2,800 rupees and insisted he had handed him 28,000 rupees. On telephone calls to his sisters, Daddykins approximated all costs to imaginary inflated sums.

In late January, tripping over words while talking into the phone, he commanded Vijaya and Saroja to join him at Samyuktha's home in Palakkad in early February. I sensed an urgency in his voice.

Perhaps he believed he would be whole again in the salubrious air that had once nourished him. Lord Gopalakrishna would clear his gullet, snip the pancreatic tumour, pump blood back into his veins and puff up his furrowed skin, leaving him once again a ruddy young boy.

I worried that Daddykins would not be able to withstand the five-day trip to Palakkad. Vinayagam theorised that unhappy ghosts wandered the earth when they had unfinished business in the mortal world. 'Amma, do you want your father's ghost roaming about on earth and haunting you?'

In the countdown to February, Daddykins made innumerable plans. He told Vinayagam that en route to Palakkad, he would sip fresh coconut water sold on the road. Vinayagam informed him he would fly, not go by road. On another morning, he said he would order Samyuktha's caterer to fry hot *appam* for him. 'You haven't eaten solids in over six months,' I reminded him gently hoping to appeal to his rational side. He turned away. 'But an *appam* is different,' he countered not wanting to accept that he couldn't even wear his dentures following the stroke. 'Fine, deprive me of that too!' he said, sullenly. It broke my heart that my father could not eat that favourite food, a sphere of sweetened rice exploding with the flavour of banana, coconut, cardamom and ghee.

Every day, Daddykins talked about experiencing *Ther*—the chariot festival—again. It was a grand spectacle at the temple of Lord Gopalakrishna: the intricately carved wooden chariot, that inch-thick, braided coir rope, the crazy crowds, the cacophony of drums, the cymbals punching the air, the chanting and the peals of laughter, the cloying sweetness of mango and jackfruit trees pendulous with fruit. We reminded my father that *Ther* was not in February but much later, in the first week of May. However, in my father's brain, time had collapsed.

One evening in early February 2014, Daddykins, Urmila and I touched down at Coimbatore airport. Vinayagam and Saravanan reached by car from Chennai. Together, we drove for ninety minutes through coconut orchards and unmapped villages on a 25-mile wide mountain pass called the Palakkad Gap.

The first morning in Palakkad, Daddykins flung a pillow at Urmila when she didn't bring him his coffee soon after he awoke. He had been unable to swallow water that morning and Vinayagam and Saravanan had sat him down on the bed and explained to him that we had to wait and watch before we deluged his system again with more fluid.

His sisters watched their brother's petulance and rage in silence. Out of earshot, they lamented the change in their stable, logical brother, their anchor for decades. He had been a good man. Why was he being tested this way? Why this hardship? The Three Roses wept. Urmila wiped her tears. My eyes welled up. Saravanan stared at the floor. Vinayagam stepped out into the porch.

A few hours later, we escorted him to the stone entrance of the temple to Lord Gopalakrishna. Bare-chested, clad in a starched white dhoti, Daddykins was as willowy as a rice sapling. The manager of the temple led him to the wooden chariot behind the temple. My father felt the smoothness of the wood, the carved *yalis*, the elephants with their legs punching the air as if in a march, the brass bells marking each consecutive level of the pyramidal chariot. He beamed through his tears. Daddykins told the manager and his siblings that he was waiting for the chariot festivities later that evening. When he was informed, once again, that *Ther* was three months later, in May, Daddykins' face fell. He returned home, fraught with disappointment.

During our stay in Palakkad, food had a natural tendency to factor into every family discussion. One evening, the conversation swung to *idi chakkai*, the raw young jackfruit that I had just bought at the farmer's market which I longed to eat steamed and seasoned with coconut flakes.

'I haven't eaten it in so long,' Daddykins said. A hush fell over us. 'Can't I have some?' my father asked, sucking in his breath, his face scanning the blank expressions of his sisters. Then he looked at Urmila. She answered in the negative again, shaking her head in slow motion. 'You have to stay healthy so you can fly back home in one piece,' she said.

All three days, Daddykins stole glances at us as we ate breakfast, lunch and dinner, averting his eyes if anyone looked up. His eyes also followed the trail of a bag that was set on the table at teatime: *bondas* and *bajjis*, a Palakkad specialty fried at many street corners that Samyuktha wanted us to taste. To Daddykins we offered a formulaic menu with the safe constants: coffee, milk and biscuit puree, clear vegetable soup, Ensure, coffee, buttermilk, tea and then Ensure again.

We steered him outside so he sat in the verandah while we ate. But the aroma of food swirled about him and us as the caterers sailed into the house. They carried short, gourd-shaped steel vessels with curved handles that opened up to freshly seasoned pumpkin sambar. Tall cylindrical containers arrived with steaming hot rice.

Rasam flowed out of a one-foot *thooku*; inside, cylindrical bits of coriander stem floated in a spicy gruel; the drift of pepper, tomato and curry leaves stung my eyes. The third evening, *lemon sevai*, my father's boyhood favourite, made its way into the kitchen. The cook had soaked, ground and steamed parboiled rice, pushing balls of it through a minuscule noodle maker. The curly ball of noodles she had steamed and seasoned with juice of lime, green chillies, curry leaves, mustard seeds, pigeon peas, powdered fenugreek and asafetida. It was eaten dipped in coconut chutney. I sensed then how my father's inability to explore those nostalgic textures had tumefied into a lump in his throat. He seemed tense one evening as he sat in front of the television. I put an arm around him and held him close. I asked him why he was glum.

'I have not accomplished what I wanted,' he said. His voice was low and raspy. 'The people I had relied on have disappointed me.' He wouldn't state their names. But it dawned on me right then that more than anything in the world, he was desperate to eat and had hoped that the Three Roses and Palakkad would effect a magical transformation in him. But in the village of his boyhood, he had finally discovered that it would not be so. The only person who could console him that night was Urmila.

The following morning, we drove down a straight path that my father had walked in his childhood, past bungalows flushed with hibiscus plants, mango clusters and billowing coconut fronds, past the Toddy Shop, past the ladies walking by in wet saris clinging to damp blouses. The path ended at the *Bharathapuzha* where Daddykins had once almost lost his life among the water hyacinths and lotuses.

We listened to crickets and crows. We heard the thrash of wet clothes on rock, the gurgle of water flowing around river plants. As we drove back, tires crunching over gravel, I imagined a youthful Daddykins hurrying back from the river after his bath, a dry, crinkled dhoti around his waist and the old wet dhoti draped around his neck like a garland.

In the evening, we drove my father to the Bhagavathi temple, which was nestled between paddy fields that had once belonged to my grandfather. The goddess had met all our ancestors for many hundred years. She had saved Daddykins many a time. My father sat down on the temple's stone bench, shirtless, as was customary, while praying to the deity, his chest lined with holy ash, and forehead spotted with sandalwood and vermilion. That evening, Daddykins seemed lighter, as if at least one of his wishes had been fulfilled.

On the last day of our trip, Daddykins visited the temple of Lord Gopalakrishna again where the manager accepted his contribution and reassured him that he would dedicate a part of a day to his name every year.

'Everything is now resolved,' Daddykins said, his crooked smile lighting up his eyes. 'I'll be back in May for the festival.' Then he turned to Urmila and Vinayagam. 'Won't I?'

And Vinayagam, who was always threatening to give him a different kind of farewell, giggled and said that it all depended on what The Absolute Being had planned for him. Urmila hastily swung around to Daddykins and said, 'But of course, we'll see. If you're in good health, why not?'

Four days after we returned from Palakkad, Daddykins insisted on being taken to the office. Vinayagam and I escorted him there and stayed with him, while he reported for a few hours of duty. He faltered as he descended the stairs outside his apartment. Inside the office, I saw how difficult it was for him to focus on a task. He couldn't wipe his mouth without help. He needed assistance walking to the car, and getting in and out of it.

The following morning, my father asked me if I would be accompanying him to the office again that day. "No," I said, looking him squarely in the eye. I told him that I didn't think it was right for him to work anymore. He was furious. As he sat down to drink his Ensure, I told him that it was time to acknowledge the reality of his frailty; I asked him if he felt it was in his or the company's best interests to tax himself in this way. He listened quietly. I left the house on an errand. When I returned two hours later, my father sent for me. As he dictated seamlessly, I typed up a letter addressed to his chairman—his own son-in-law.

Chennai
Feb 11, 2014

Subject: Resignation from the post of Director

Dear Chairman:
In lieu of the recent and protracted illness, I feel drained in strength and energy. I therefore desire to submit my resignation to your company with effect from the forenoon of 1 March 2014. Please accept my resignation.

I take this opportunity to thank you for your kindness in appointing me as a director in April 1993 and allowing me to continue for the last twenty years.

I enjoyed my work and I hope you too feel that I was useful to your organisation. I wish you all the best in all your endeavors.

Thanking you,
Yours truly,
L. V. Anantram

My father practiced his signature three times on an old newspaper. Then he signed the letter. He never talked about the office again.

Shortly thereafter, I had to return to the United States. Daddykins' body shrivelled with Chennai's rising mercury. Bindu was assigned to another patient. Nameless nurses began trooping through our home. In the closing days of May, his throat sealed itself shut. Now, Daddykins could not drink water.

29

The End of a Beginning

Veedu varai uravu
Veedhi varai manaivi
Kaadu varai pillai
Kadaisi varai yaro?

~ Tamil Poet Kannadasan, 1962

All relationships end with the home
Your wife sees you off at the gate of your home
Your son bids you farewell at the crematorium
But in the end of all ends, who will be with you?

~ ~ ~

I returned to Chennai on a June morning. Daddykins wanted to go home that day and every day after that.

'This is your home,' we said.

'Take me home.'

'This is your home, Daddykins.'

He wanted his valet by his side. 'Vinayagam!' The young man did not hear. He pretended to not hear sometimes. All of us did. Life leaks out of those who care for a dying man.

I sat by my father's side in the middle of the bed. 'Baby,' Daddykins said to me, touching my arm. 'Why won't you take me home? Please.'

'Because this is your home. This is your bedroom, Daddykins,' I said. I pointed to his almirah. 'Remember, this is where you stood all these years, writing your accounts.'

He followed my finger. Then he turned to the door where sunlight streamed in.

'Saravanan!' A feeble call. But Saravanan always heard. He responded every single time. At night he ran in when Daddykins shifted slightly in bed.

'Yes, *Saar*.'

'Let's go. We need to leave this building.'

'We'll go, *Saar*,' Saravanan said. 'When Vinayagam shows up this morning, I promise you we'll go.'

Daddykins closed his eyes.

'How about you sleep now for a bit?' He turned my father over gently onto his right side. Daddykins lay in silence.

A while later, the hospice nurse on duty fiddled with the tube that snaked out of his belly as she started his feed. 'I want to go home,' Daddykins told her. She must have heard him. She went back to her chair a few feet away. She fished out her cell phone.

The day after, Urmila asked Daddykins where 'home' was. 'Parthasarathypuram?'

A light seemed to flicker. 'Yes.'

'But remember you sold our bungalow twenty years ago?' she said, pulling his hand to her cheek. 'And then you bought this flat right next to Jeeva Park.'

He pulled his hand away. 'Let's go. I'm tired.'

Later, Vinayagam brought a quarter cup of warm milk 'Feed your dad a little something,' he said to Urmila. 'Something before you fly out, Amma. Who knows?' She wetted Daddykins' tongue with a little milk. 'No sugar?' Daddykins asked. Everyone laughed. She sweetened the milk and tried again. Urmila told him she was flying to Singapore to see her newborn grandson who would take Daddykins' name. Daddykins wished her bon voyage. He rested his hand on her shoulder. 'Best wishes.' She took leave of him. He took leave of her.

The next day, he looked towards the bedroom door as he lay in a stupor. 'Let's go home,' he said, again. Mid-morning, Vinayagam held him on one side, Saravanan on the other. Daddykins panted to the living room and back, dragging both his feet. A slip of a man swollen in his stomach, his feet, his legs, his hands.

'Please write letters to my three sisters in Coimbatore. Their father will not last long. He'll be breathing his last tomorrow.' Who was brother? Who was father? But the love? That was the same. He seemed to lapse into his world of darkness. I believe, however, that for the briefest moment, he entered mine. 'My brothers are no more,' he said.

'Yes, I know, Daddykins.'

'Carry me.'

'Where are you? In Chennai or in Palakkad?'

'Palakkad.'

The next day he was drowsy all day and all night. We made his feed. 6, 8, 10, 12, 2, 4, 6, 8, 10. Even feeds in. Odd man out. Peptamen milk. Sweat. Fever. Chills. Panadol. Heat. Air-conditioning. Pan 40. Strocit. Stator. Diaper. Wet wipes. Peptamen milk. Sweat. Fever. Diaper. Wet wipes. Heat. Air-conditioning. Wet bed.

The nurse lifted her mask. Vinayagam opened the balcony doors. He turned the fan on high. Saravanan tied the garbage bag. 'Let's dump it right away.'

Was it green?

It was dark green, almost black.

The smell of death.

The day after, Daddykins could not stand. His feet buckled. When we sat him on the chair, his torso and his head caved to the right, unseeing, like his wife's nine years before. He sat there in his white cotton vest on his white diaper—almost dead in life but a newborn in death.

The scent of a newborn. Vertically opposite in the circle called life.

* * *

On Saturday, the day before Father's Day, Urmila, Thalaivar and the Three Roses flew in to be at his bedside. Daddykins floated in and out of two worlds, neither here nor there, in the lair of the living and in the den of the dead. He was at the threshold, the place where no one may linger, the place where strokes made his body thrash, where entrails could be pulled and twisted even by a god so kind as Lord Gopalakrishna.

I still had so much left to say to my father. I longed to tell him how excited India was about a new prime minister. I hoped to tell him that Nadal won the tennis grand slam for the fourteenth time. I yearned to tell him how we had missed watching FIFA's opening in Brazil. I wanted him to realise that no one in the house turned on the television any longer—not even Vinayagam, with his penchant for old movie songs in which mustachioed heroes cavorted with women with cone-shaped breasts. I wished to give my father the day's unopened newspaper. 'This, here, is fresh off the press,' I wanted to say. 'Take in the smell of the paper. Feel its crease.'

On Father's Day, forty minutes after midnight—while we paced outside his room, worrying about his breathing—Daddykins drifted away, like cotton from the kapok tree, through the air-conditioning unit, the balcony, or the bathroom window perhaps. A few hours after his final exhalation, the late Daddykins' kitchen scissors with the orange handle severed in two.

* * *

Muniyamma, from the nursing home around the corner, had visited Daddykins two days prior to nebulize him. She had arrived in a starched white uniform, stiff skirt, white stockings and cap. Florence Nightingale with a red bindi on her forehead.

In the wee hours after Daddykins' passing, Muniyamma again schlepped in, bleary-eyed, in an orange nightie.

Daddykins' body was warm to the touch. Muniyamma pressed on his eyeballs, as if she were kneading dough. She grabbed his wrist. She clipped the oxygen monitor to his thumb. She fit the blood pressure cuff around his arm. When she was done, she let his hand crash onto the bed.

At the dining table, she heaved her body into the chair.

'What was the old man's name?'

I wrote it down.

She showed me a menu of illnesses. 'And how did he die?'

I pointed to one and handed back the paper. 'I believe he died from a cardiopulmonary arrest.'

She nodded. She told Vinayagam that the death certificate would be ready at 9.30 AM.

***

'I cannot tell Urmila. She will be upset,' Daddykins had said to me. 'But you I can tell. I don't want anyone to see my crooked mouth. On that day, tie my face.'

***

They cleaned the body. Vinayagam tied his boss's face tight at 1 AM. 'Tighter', Thalaiver said. Vinayagam hesitated, holding the cloth in his hands. Thalaivar gestured as if to say, 'You can.' But the mouth stayed crooked. By 5 AM, with plenty of time to spare before visitors started arriving, Daddykins was no more the man with the crooked mouth.

***

The priest told Urmila and me to stand under running water. Then he bade us wash our father. Urmila the eldest, from his head to toe. Me, the younger one, from his toe to head. Then the late Daddykins lay on a wooden cot as Thalaivar prepped him for his last journey through town to the burning ghat in West Mambalam. Now draped in a new dhoti with a zari border, looking most regal, the late Daddykins was carried, past his rust-orange sofa, out of his living room. Out past his door. Out beyond the shoe cabinet on which he used to sit when he returned from Jeeva Park. Down the eighteen steps. Down the verandah by which a Honda motorcycle always stood. They loaded him into the back of a van, legs first.

Tutenkhamen in a dhoti. Leaving behind his wallet. Leaving behind his glasses. Leaving behind his dentures. Leaving us behind.

The late Daddykins' hearse turned away from Jeeva Park, past Nalli's where the missus exchanged everything at least three times, past Panagal Park where he bought Urmila roasted peanuts in a cone, past Universal Stores where he bought me butter cookies, past the 11A bus-stop where, daily, Vinayagam once awaited a bus home to Porur, and then once again past the ghost of Doctor's old bungalow where he learned to start a life.

At the ghat, Thalaivar and Daddykins' girls fed him rice, curd, honey and milk. Thalaivar set a burning cow patty in the middle of the late Daddykins' chest.

A fire now where once a flame burned.

* * *

Into the open-mouthed fire.
To the chant of *Govinda, Govinda, Narayana, Narayana.*
Who is none but Lord Gopalakrishna.
Burn. Splutter. Rage. Old Man Frying. Young Man Crying.
A man Friday fleeing the fire, back turned to the Sunday pyre.
Sobbing. Once a boy of 18. Now a man of 35.
A young man who then led an old man to the bank.
A young man who now led an old man to the other bank.
Bones. Ash. The Remains of the Day.
Little bones. Gravely bones. Big bones.

Water over baked bones. Cool bones.
Pick your bones. None left to pick.

***

'Madam, you don't know me. I just saw the obituary in *The Hindu* this morning. Your father was my boss from 1956 to 1959. I'll never forget his encouragement and his kindness. One tiny remark from him set the tone for my career and the rest of my life, you know? I was typing up a report that morning. He passed me by. He said, 'Srinivasan, you know typing *too*?' How can I ever forget that word 'too'? I suppose it was a small observation on his part but in the way LV-Sir—we all called him LV-Sir, you know—said it, he did not ever behave as if typing were an ordinary thing. He looked upon it as a valuable skill and he appreciated me for the talent that I possessed. I was just a superintendent then but sixty years later I still remember how special he made me feel that day. He's the sole reason I set high goals for myself and excelled even after I left the A. G's office. I'm so sad today. Please accept my heartfelt condolences. He was a great man.'

***

On the fourteenth day after Daddykins' passing, the sun charred the ends of gulmohar blossoms turned upwards. Vinayagam wondered when the heavens would quench the earth.

The air conditioner whirred in the bedrooms and in the living room. Vinayagam admonished me. 'Have you considered the bills we're going to get, Amma?'

'It hardly matters,' I said. 'Daddykins isn't ever going to turn on the lights in our house anymore, is he?' Vinayagam's face fell. He turned around and marched back into the kitchen.

The sky brooded that evening. We ran upstairs to the terrace to recover our drying clothes. A zephyr hissed through our manjadi tree. Raindrops clattered on our terrace.

The next morning, Daddykins' two friends and I walked together round and round Jeeva Park to the chant, over the speakers, of the *Gayatri mantra* that my father had recited every morning and every evening.

Om buhr bhuva swaha tat savitur varenyam
bhargo devasya dheemahi dhiyo yonaha prachodayat

We meditate on the effulgent glory of the divine Sun,
the god of light; may he illuminate our minds

I walked back to Daddykins' apartment. Up in the kapok tree, cotton balls hung pendulously now, their ends pointy. Water bags, about to birth something new into the air. A squirrel sprinted down a cable TV wire. Pigeons tap-danced on our neighbor's roof. Manjadi pods had exploded inside our building, disseminating red beads all around.

At 7.30 AM, Vinayagam walked up to the framed photograph from inside which Daddykins now surveyed everyone who walked into his house. 'It's June 30, *Saar*,' he said to him. 'That paper is sitting there unfolded, unread. Where are you, *Saar*?' Daddykins stared out from his '8 by 10' window, looking dapper in his blue cotton shirt and, as always, sporting his crooked smile.

Later, oats made, prayer alcove cleaned, at 8.30 AM, Vinayagam crossed the living room to sit down on the cool marble floor by the side of Daddykins' rust-orange sofa right behind the glass table. 'Amma, enjoy *The Hindu* today. Remember, from tomorrow we won't be getting the newspaper anymore. You're flying out too, remember?' He disappeared behind the day's *Dina Thandhi*.

***

Vinayagam came into the kitchen on a July morning. He told me his wife had dreamed of Daddykins and that he too had been thinking of him so much the previous evening.

'But you have no idea how I feel when I return home in the evening. I feel I have no one to turn to for a solution to the challenges in my life. I would come to *Saar* for solace. We all need one person like that in our lives. Someone we go to that we trust, who has the experience, who will not talk down to us, who knows us well enough to give us simple, practical solutions to our life problems. He was that person for me.'

He washed the rice under running water. 'It didn't hit me upon his death. There were the logistics of the cremation, the people pouring in to talk to us, the rites for thirteen days, the conversations with you, Thalaivar, Urmila-Amma and the Three Roses, the phone calls and all that running around.' He shut off the tap and set the rice container down.

'But now I'm hurting.' I could hear the wetness of his tears in his voice. 'From here on, I have no one like that in my life.'

He wrung a washcloth dry and began wiping the counter.

Then he paused, turning to me. 'Amma, just where do you think he is? Like, right now?' He didn't wait for me to answer. 'I bet he's out there somewhere in the universe being reborn. You know, two days after he passed away, my friend at the office told me not to worry. '*Saar* will be reborn,' he said. I'm telling you. *Saar* will be reborn. As your child.' He laughed. He wiped his eyes.

'You, mister,' I said, stirring in two spoons of ghee into the bubbling pot of water, 'you are going to be my father's boss—even in his next life?'

All of a sudden, my mind spawned ideas like tadpoles in an algae-filled pond. '*Aieiii,* on the other hand,' I said in a volte-face, turning to look at him, my arms akimbo. 'If Daddykins were reborn as your child, you will be slave and he will be master!' I said, with a shriek. 'Finally!' Vinayagam and I began cackling like a pair of laughing hyenas. The late Daddykins' home returned to its temporary state of a contrived normalcy.

***

In December, Vinayagam drove our family to the shore temples at Mahabalipuram. We ambled about the old rocks that had been chiseled by the passage of time. From the doorway of the main temple, I urged my children to look at the stone bench on which their grandfather had sat many moons before. Daddykins had cut a slight figure against the sun and the sea. For a second, I thought I caught the flutter of his shawl. I told my children then about the ancient stone lion that had roared in from the sea after the last tsunami. An old truth seemed to wash up over and over among these ruins, that a force infinitely larger than us shaped the stories of our lives.